LATE-BLOOMING ENTREPRENEURS

EIGHT PRINCIPLES FOR STARTING A BUSINESS AFTER AGE 40

LYNNE BEVERLY STRANG

Late-Blooming Entrepreneurs:
Eight Principles for Starting a Business After Age 40
By Lynne Beverly Strang

Portions of this book previously appeared on
www.latebloomingentrepreneurs.wordpress.com/

Cover, layout and interior design by Damonza.com

Edited by Nancy McKeon

Published by:
White Chimney Press
P.O. Box 156
Clifton, VA 20124

Printed in the United States of America

ISBN: 978-0-9899803-2-6

Disclaimer

For my father, who designed buildings and remained passionate about his work until the end.

CONTENTS

WHY BECOME A LATE-BLOOMING ENTREPRENEUR?

"People sometimes ask me why I'm still working. I'm working because I'm not good at retirement. I love what I'm doing."

– Bill Cheeks, ABBA Associates

"Each day is so precious. Tomorrow you never know. If you don't try it, you may ask in the future: Why didn't I take that opportunity?"

– Grace Welch, Patemm

"Age, by itself, doesn't determine successful entrepreneurship but it offers some very real advantages in the business world. By the time you're 40, you understand what it takes to make a life. You're dealing with REALITY, not fantasy, and potentially have a more accurate assessment of yourself and the environment."

– Elizabeth Erlandson, Licorice International

"For me, it felt like I couldn't be myself when I was working for someone else. I didn't want to compromise my integrity."

— Michael Penny, Savvy Rest

"Looking back, there weren't many options. I was over-educated, too old and needed a creative job. I had been making decisions and wasn't going to have someone start making them for me."

— Barbara Cosgrove, Barbara Cosgrove Lamps

"I had spent my career in high-powered corporate-marketing positions. When my dad — who was my mentor and closest friend — became seriously ill, I went to see him. I asked myself: 'If this were my last day on Earth, is this what I would want to be doing?' "

— Franny Martin, Cookies on Call

"After more than 25 years in the corporate culture, I knew there had to be a better way of running a business."

— Richard Urban, Card Alert Services

"After I left my nursing career, I discovered that being creative is what really makes me happy. Entrepreneurship lets me apply that creativity and contribute to the culture of fashion in my own small way. When you can do what you love and still be relevant later in life, that's truly a blessing."

— Annie Margulis, Girls Golf

"It was never about the money. It was about the challenge and the accomplishment."

— Sharon Dillard, Get A Grip

"I like that quote by CS Lewis: 'You're never too old to set another goal or to dream another dream.'"

— Donna Herrle, Drawing Conclusions

PREFACE

Can a boomer make it as an entrepreneur? You'd better believe it! Look around and you'll find plenty of examples.

Some of the most admired business owners fall into the late bloomer category. Margaret Rudkin was a 40-year-old homemaker when she started Pepperidge Farm. Ray Kroc was in his 50s when McDonald's took off. And then there's Colonel Sanders. By the time he launched Kentucky Fried Chicken, he was well into his 60s!

Between 1996 and 2012, the share of new U.S. entrepreneurs in the 55-to-64 age group grew from 14.3 percent to 23.4 percent, says the Ewing Marion Kauffman Foundation, the largest American foundation to focus on entrepreneurship. Today, baby boomers are becoming business owners like never before.

At an age once considered "over the hill," these late bloomers run successful online businesses, brick-and-mortar operations, consulting practices and franchises. They invent products and do business all over the world. In many cases, they earn more money now than they did working for someone else.

How did they do it? What advice do they have for those of us who are past 40 – and still harbor the Great American Dream of owning a business? What does it take to succeed as a late-blooming entrepreneur? That's what this book is about.

To research it, I interviewed marketing experts, lenders, personal coaches and midlife career changers. I also drew upon personal experience gained from my own transition – from a public relations executive to a writer/communications consultant – and the front-row seat I had when my husband Jim founded a retail bicycle business in the 1980s.

Most of the material, however, comes from dozens of interviews with men and women who own (or owned) businesses but didn't start them until they were in their 40s, 50s, 60s or later. After all, who better to advise aspiring entrepreneurs of a certain age than people who have been there?

Some of the featured entrepreneurs started businesses within familiar industries. Others, however, made remarkable transitions. Among them: a retired nurse who created an international golf clothing line; a one-time flight attendant who has a computer security firm; a former yoga instructor who heads an organic mattress company; and a retired grocery chain executive with a pond-supplies business.

In this book, you'll find eight basic principles used by these entrepreneurs to start and operate successful businesses later in life. Not every entrepreneur applied each principle but, collectively, the eight present a foundation that can help aspiring or new business owners.

If you long to join their ranks, I hope this book inspires you to take action. While their accomplishments are impressive, the late-blooming entrepreneurs you are about to meet are not superheroes. They made it happen through hard work, tenacity and other tried-and-true fundamentals. If they can do it, so can you.

Lynne Strang

CHAPTER 1
GO OUT ON THE RIGHT LIMB

Why would a man is his 40s walk away from a well-paying executive position to start a limousine service? Here's a story about Rory Kelly, who did just that.

For Rory, the allure of limos – and a dream of owning one – took hold when he was just five years old. You might think it was because he wanted to chauffeur celebrities and other VIPs, but young Rory had someone else in mind. "I wanted one," he said, "to drive my grandmother around."

Like many people, Rory put his dream behind him and went on with life. He graduated from West Virginia University with a degree in marketing, then went to work in the steel piling industry as an inside sales representative. During a 26-year career, he climbed the corporate ladder, holding a series of management positions and acquiring knowledge in budgeting, human resources and other areas needed to run a company.

Eventually, he became Vice President of Operations

for a steel foundation supplier owned by the world's largest steel company. His job responsibilities grew after Enron Corporation's 2001 collapse, an event that prompted the federal government to impose new restrictions on all publicly traded companies, including those in the steel industry. "I became the internal compliance person and, as a result, I wasn't liked by my coworkers," Rory said.

Despite this uncomfortable situation, he stayed with the company and produced at a level that earned him bonuses – all of which he stashed away in savings. Finally, he reached a point where he'd had enough. "I wanted out of the steel business because it wasn't fun anymore," said Rory.

In 2004, Mary Kelly – aware of her husband's childhood dream – bought him a special birthday present: a limousine. The new set of wheels provided a fun way to get around. But it also was the catalyst for something bigger.

Two years later, when he was 48, Rory Kelly left his job to launch a limousine business. As Rory explained, he and Mary chose the name Prestige Limousine because "it reflected the kind of business we wanted to be and the type of service we wanted to provide."

So far, Fairfax, Virginia-based Prestige Limousine LLC seems to be living up to its moniker. The company's revenue rose 40 percent between 2007 and 2013, a performance that "has exceeded expectations," said Rory. About 50 to 60 percent of Prestige Limo's work comes from providing backup services for a core group of 10 other limo companies in the Washington, D.C. area. The remaining 40 percent of its clientele, which ranges from business executives to brides, comes from word-of-mouth advertising or referrals.

"I get satisfaction in knowing I found a need and filled it, which is a basic marketing principle," Rory added. "I also enjoy seeing employees become enthusiastic about the business, which generates goodwill towards customers."

Best of all, Rory's childhood dream finally came true. He now spends most of his days driving a shiny, elegant limousine!

Rory Kelly could have taken "the safe route" by staying in his job and continuing to receive the bonuses and other perks that come with an executive position. But he didn't because, as he put it, he wasn't having fun anymore. Instead, he opted to realize his dream – a decision that required him to relinquish job security and take a risk.

Frankly, most people wouldn't have made the same decision as Rory, in part because they wouldn't have had the guts. A 2009 Ewing Marion Kauffman

Foundation report asked 549 company founders about factors that may prevent others from starting their own businesses. The factor most commonly ranked as important was "lack of willingness or of ability to take risk," with 98 percent of the participants saying it was an important factor.[1]

The company founders answered this way for a good reason: Risk is inherent in business ownership. It never goes away, even for established, serial entrepreneurs who have made millions of dollars.

A willingness to take risks doesn't mean you have to accept *all* risks, however. Actually, it's the opposite. To succeed as a business owner, you don't go out on a limb. You go out on the *right* limb. That involves adopting an approach followed by Rory Kelly and others – which is to select certain risks and avoid others.

CALCULATED VERSUS FOOLISH RISKS

George S. Patton is one of the most celebrated generals in American history. Among his best-known quotes is this one: "Take calculated risks. That is quite different from being rash."

Apparently, many business leaders think the same way as the general. The U.S. Small Business Administration's list of typical traits for successful entrepreneurs includes "calculated risk taker,"[2] which describes most of the people in this book. Once they found a viable business opportunity, they weighed, or calculated, the risks and possible results (both positive and negative) before deciding to move forward.

"You have to think of everything," said Rory Kelly, who devoted two years to learning about the limousine business before finally making his move. "A business entails small and large details, as well as all aspects of your life, so think it through thoroughly."

How do successful entrepreneurs like Rory determine which risks are worth taking? They go with the ones that have a higher probability of producing rewards. That requires basing their decisions on *thorough research,* rather than whims or untested assumptions.

In that respect, the process isn't all that different from gauging the risks associated with other major life decisions. Just as you wouldn't (or shouldn't) buy a seemingly good house without a careful evaluation first, the same thing is true about starting a business.

"It's important to read, read, read," said Bill Cheeks, an entrepreneur in the financial literacy field. "Understand the fundamentals of operating a business and what's going on in your industry. I have so much reading in those two areas that I have almost no time to read anything else."

When Donna Herrle decided to open her own graphic design company, her decision wasn't based on assumptions. As a single mother of two sons, she couldn't afford to take that kind of a risk.

For eight years, Donna worked at a health-care-group purchasing organization in Pittsburgh. In addition to a degree in graphic design, she had management experience and expertise in sales marketing, websites and printing. She also had a part-time freelance business, dubbed Drawing Conclusions, that she started several years ago as a way to stay involved in what she loved the most: designing.

Her transition to full-time entrepreneurship began when she received a layoff slip with only two days' notice. The news came two weeks before her 50th birthday.

Her first reaction was shock. But once she regrouped, Donna began to see the layoff in a different light. She recognized it was an opportunity to use her professional credentials in a new, exciting way.

"I asked myself: Do I want another corporate job?

Or do I want to do design on a full-time basis?" said Donna.

It was a huge decision – especially for Donna who, as a single parent, didn't have the safety net of a spouse's income or job benefits (like health insurance). What followed was a series of informational interviews and an assessment of the positives and risks associated with business ownership.

Recognizing the need for family support, the first people she spoke to were her two sons. They gave their wholehearted endorsement for converting Drawing Conclusions into a full-fledged design company (her oldest son also provides IT, back-office and other support for the business).

Donna sought feedback from as many professional colleagues and business owners as she could on whether she had "what it takes" to succeed. They, too, encouraged her to go out on her own, noting that her previous sales marketing experience would help her find business.

She also spoke with her freelance clients to gauge their future need for her services. Those conversations showed that she would be able to start her new business with five or six clients, ensuring income right from the beginning.

Based upon her research, Donna followed her heart. In October 2002, she incorporated as a full-time entity. The company started with a grand opening party that netted new work, plus an International Gold Quill Award from the International Association of Business Communicators for the party invitation designed by Donna. Within the first six months, her list of clients grew to 60.

Today, Drawing Conclusions – whose website says it "offers graphic design with direction"– has around 100 clients, six to eight subcontracted employees and annual revenue in the six figures. Its design work includes websites, brochures, direct mail, annual reports and tradeshow material as well as advertising and logo creation.

Back when she was a stay-at home mother, Donna never expected to become an entrepreneur. Now she enjoys being her own boss. "When I was working in a full-time job, it was a bit discouraging when people didn't get promoted when they deserved to be," she said. "The appeal of business ownership is that no one determines my success but me."

WHAT ABOUT LUCK?

Donna Herrle's approach to risk exemplifies that followed by other entrepreneurs. They often reach out and tap the expertise of others to help them make the right decisions. As a result, they "stack the deck" in their favor and don't have to depend as much on chance.

"Hard work, non-compromising quality and luck have an awful lot to do with success," said Franny Martin, a Michigan entrepreneur who sells freshly baked cookies and other treats online and through several storefronts. "In my case, I was fortunate to meet the right people at the right time, who gave me the right advice."

Many of the entrepreneurs interviewed for this book feel the same way. The right people or the right opportunities "just came along," they said. The old adage "the harder I work, the luckier I get" applies to these entrepreneurs, but they also are smart enough to recognize and grab opportunities that present themselves.

In addition, they take initiatives that allow luck to find *them*. The International Gold Quill Award, for example, didn't just drop into Donna Herrle's lap. She made it possible by submitting an entry form for the award, along with a work plan that included measurements to demonstrate the success of her grand opening party invitation.

"You put yourself out there and that's the luck," said Barbara Cosgrove, an artist who became a commercial and home lighting business owner. "You have to be open to other possibilities constantly."

Without question, Barbara and the others *take advantage of the possibilities* brought by luck. That doesn't mean, however, they *depend* upon luck. In other words, they don't take risks or make decisions about starting businesses based on the hope or belief they will get lucky.

Business blogger Paul Morin addressed this subject in a post that asked, "Are Entrepreneurs Gamblers?" The answer is no, in his opinion. A gambler, wrote Morin, "is someone who places bets, hoping to win by chance, usually against the odds." Yet their odds of winning are almost zero, since they're playing against the house (the casino).[3]

Maybe those odds are acceptable if you want to have fun at the blackjack table and can deal with losing. But when it comes to a business startup, "hoping to win by chance" is a foolish risk, to say the least.

POTENTIAL RISKS FACED BY OLDER ENTREPRENEURS

Most risks associated with entrepreneurship have nothing to do with age. No matter how old you are, you can't predict or control certain external events, like an economy that goes south or weather conditions that keep people from buying. Until you begin operating your startup, you also can't say, for sure, if you'll be able to contain costs, create sufficient market demand, outperform competitors, find the right employees or overcome a host of other obstacles faced by all business owners.

But the reality is that aspiring entrepreneurs past the age of 40 have different circumstances – and different bodies – from those in their 20s and 30s. As a result, a few aged-related risk factors may enter into the picture, such as:

HEALTH

The older you get, the more prone you become to health issues – and the better the chance of a medical event that keeps you from working.

While everyone needs health insurance, entrepreneurs with insufficient coverage assume an especially significant risk. If you become sick or injured, exorbitant medical bills can wipe out your business *and* your personal assets, creating a double whammy.

Health insurance may not be a problem, especially if a spouse is working and has a policy, or you're fortunate enough to have retired from a job that provides lifetime coverage. But for single and/ or cash-strapped entrepreneurs, the premiums can create the temptation to buy the cheapest coverage possible – or forgo health insurance altogether.

The takeaway here is to make sure you have adequate health insurance before going out on your own. And if you haven't had a physical in a while, now is a good time to get one, so you'll know where you stand health-wise.

STAMINA

Although many of this book's entrepreneurs were well into their 50s and 60s when interviewed, none mentioned their health as an obstacle for their start-ups. Since these business owners enjoy what they're doing, it could be that their positive mental state manifests itself in fewer physical problems. It's also possible they wouldn't have pursued entrepreneurship in the first place if they had been hindered by health complications.

Most like to walk, jog, ride a bike, play golf or go to the gym. But even when they don't exercise regularly, their mental focus lets them tune out physical ailments. "If my back starts to hurt, I pretend it doesn't," said Cookies on Call's Franny Martin.

Yet for many people, entrepreneurship's long hours, minimal sleep and mental stress can be wearing. That presents a consideration for aspiring older entrepreneurs, who need to think about whether they have the physical and mental endurance for what lies ahead.

"Sleep deprivation affects 40-and-older entrepreneurs more than younger ones because their reaction and decision-making time already is slower because of age," said Patti Hudson, a life coach who leads workshops on health, stress management and other topics related to work/life balance.

Like health, insufficient stamina wasn't an obstacle for the interviewed entrepreneurs, in part because they know how to manage themselves.

"I've always been a high-energy person," said Suzanne Magee, who co-owns a cybersecurity company. "But it's good to take breaks and give yourself time to think. I also get up early and go to bed early." Before bedtime, Suzanne separates herself mentally from the business day's events by doing a crossword puzzle or reading a newspaper.

"I've probably lost a step but I try to counteract that by working smarter," said Bill McKechnie, an entrepreneur in the restaurant industry. "I wish I had the same energy I had at 20 but would not trade the experience I've gained."

Some interviewed entrepreneurs believe their age gives them *more* stamina. Even if their physical strength isn't what it used to be, grit, passion and a clear vision keep them going through difficult times. Chapter 6, "Stay on the Tiger," talks about this in more detail.

LOSS OF RETIREMENT FUNDS

When it comes to age-related risks, the biggest one – by far – is blowing retirement money. Art Koff, the creator of RetiredBrains.com, knows this, which is why his website devotes extensive space to financial resources and planning advice. People in their 50s and 60s "are a little bit more loath" to take financial risks, said Art.

It's easy to understand why, especially if you're someone who has contributed to a 401(k) or IRA faithfully over the years. The possibility of losing some, or all, of that hard-earned money needed for the Golden Years is enough for some people to avoid entrepreneurship altogether.

The only way to avert this risk entirely is to leave your retirement funds out of the business. That's what David Drewry did.

David is the former president of Drewry Home Inspections (DHI), a family-owned and operated business in Haymarket, Virginia that provides professional home inspection services for new and previously owned homes in the Northern Virginia area.

He estimates that the company has done between 15,000 and 20,000 inspections since its start in the late 1980s.

For many years, David and his son, Mark, handled the home inspections while his wife, Anna, was the office manager. When David and Anna retired in January 2013, Mark and his wife, Christy, took over the business.

Born in Tennessee and raised in Mississippi, David has come a long way from his self-described days as "an LD [Learning Disability] student who was more interested in working." After three years of mediocre grades at a local community college, he transferred to Mississippi State University, where he changed his degree from engineering to Industrial Arts Education and became an A/B student.

Upon graduation, David had 26 offers to teach shop. Instead, he went to graduate school, earning a Master of Education in Industrial, Vocational and Technical Education from Mississippi State in 1966. He then joined the U.S. Air Force, where he received his commission as a second lieutenant one year later. A 21-year military career took him to Japan, Korea, Turkey and Thailand, among other places.

By 1988, he was a lieutenant colonel stationed in Indian Head, Maryland. When a promotion to colonel didn't materialize, he decided to retire from the military. As he pondered the next chapter in his life, he considered teaching but didn't want to start from the ground floor again. "I had a choice," said David. "I could utilize post-military training to find my next career or do something different."

He opted for the latter largely because of two Air Force contacts, both former military officers who had gone into real estate. They recognized his aptitude for the home inspection business and encouraged him to go that route. David thought it was a good fit as well.

In August 1988, he founded Drewry Home Inspections at the age of 45. As a business owner, David enjoyed cultivating long-term relationships and "the feeling that I provided a service that people appreciate." He credits his success to the discipline he learned from the military, along with the application of its principles. Among them: be aboveboard, professional, reliable and timely.

In addition, his time spent in the Air Force gave him something else: a pension. Along with other entrepreneurs featured in these pages, David was careful to keep this income separate from his business. Some business owners lack the discipline to implement this approach but – given his military background – David isn't one of them. "My own comfort level would not have been as high without military retirement," he said.

A Shorter Time Horizon

One reason why blowing retirement money is a big concern has to do with another reality: No one lives forever – but thanks to advancements in medicine and technology, people *are* living longer.

If you're a 50-year-old man, your average life expectancy is 29 more years, says the U.S. Census Bureau. If you're a woman of the same age, it's almost 33 more years.[4] That's a big chunk of time in which to start a business, especially if you stay in reasonably good health like most of the late bloomers featured in this book.

Still, an entrepreneur who is 50 or 60 doesn't have the same time window as one who is 20 or 30. That translates into greater business risk for two reasons. One, you have less time to recoup any personal funds used for startup capital. And two, you don't have as many years to grow the business into a success, or to start another one if the first doesn't work out.

And remember: It isn't just about you, especially if you have a 40-or-older significant other with a limited time window as well. You have to consider how the uncertainty will affect family members, which Chapter 3 covers in more detail.

AGE DISCRIMINATION

Happily, none of the interviewed owners mentioned age discrimination as an impediment to their businesses – and virtually all of them saw their age as a positive factor, rather than a negative one. But for older entrepreneurs seeking venture capital, age bias is a possibility – at least in the technical field.

Technology investor Seth Levine is among those who have commented on this topic. In a blog post, Levine recounted his reactions during a pitch meeting with three tech entrepreneurs in their late 40s to early 50s.

"Certainly there is some amount of age bias in venture. Early-stage tech is considered somewhat of a young person's game," wrote Levine. "And while I've worked with many very experienced entrepreneurs who were and are fantastic, I wonder if the initial pangs of question I felt on entering a room with three, middle-aged guys in suits pitching me their business plan is something that is deeper than a momentary hesitation."[5]

THE REAL VALUE OF A BUSINESS PLAN

Age-related considerations are just some of the potential risks to think about, of course. The next chapter shows how a self-evaluation can unearth personal weaknesses – such as a tendency to procrastinate or poor communications skills – that could derail your business idea. But identifying the risks isn't enough, say many established owners. You also need a plan that details how you'll *address* those risks.

"No other steps can be, or need be, taken until you have a business plan in writing," said Prestige Limousine's Rory Kelly. "This will keep you on track to growth."

So what, exactly, *is* a business plan? The U.S. Small Business Administration defines it as "a living document" that generally projects three to five years in advance and "outlines the route a company intends to take to grow revenues."[6] Typically, it includes several sections, such as an executive summary, a company description, a market analysis, an overview of the organization's management and financial projections, to name a few.

While most of the entrepreneurs interviewed for this book prepared a written plan, a few didn't. One said she didn't have "the luxury," as clients started requesting her services before she could prepare one. Another decided to "map" her business idea in her head because she wanted to get going on it right away.

As these two cases show, it *is* possible to get by without a written business plan. Before you breathe a sigh of relief, recognize that "possible" isn't the same as "advisable." And for some people, a plan may *not* be optional.

Chances are you'll need one to borrow money from a bank or attract outside investors (more on that subject later). It also may be a must if your proposed business involves selling merchandise, since many suppliers won't work with you without a plan that shows you know what you're doing.

That was the situation for my husband, Jim, when he decided to open his first retail bicycle store. He needed a business plan to approach bicycle companies about the possibility of becoming an authorized dealer for their product lines. Without a commitment from at least one major manufacturer, he would have little to sell when he opened his doors. Faced with that reality, we spent many evenings developing a plan at our dining room table (the makeshift hub of the startup operation for the first few months).

Even if you don't have suppliers, bankers or

others insisting on a business plan, write one anyway, say those who've been through the process. Drawing Conclusion's Donna Herrle, for example, described it as "incredibly helpful" because it gave her focus and peace of mind. "It was my psychological home," she said.

Donna's view is one often heard by SCORE, a nonprofit that provides mentors and other help for entrepreneurs and small business owners (close to 60 percent of its clients are at least 45 years old). SCORE offers online templates that walk through the process of creating a plan. On its website, the organization points out that "the real value of creating a business plan is not in having the finished product in hand; rather, the value lies in the process of researching and thinking about your business in a systematic way."[7]

Why does this reduce the risk associated with a business startup? "The act of planning helps you think things through thoroughly, study and research if you are not sure of the facts, and look at your ideas critically," says SCORE. "It takes time now, but avoids costly, perhaps disastrous, mistakes later."[8]

That last line really gets to the heart of it. Some people balk at the idea of spending weeks or months on a plan that's likely to sit on a shelf or a computer hard drive. But that's not why you're putting yourself through this process.

The true value lies in the critical thinking required to write a business plan – and the action steps taken to prevent problems *before* you encounter them. It's like the old Scout motto – Be Prepared – which goes a long way towards reducing risk. With a written business plan, you're less likely to be kicking yourself for overlooking some factor or detail that proves insurmountable later.

OTHER WAYS TO MITIGATE RISK

- *Segue into entrepreneurship*. That's what Prestige Limousine's Rory Kelly did. As mentioned earlier, he stayed at his steel-industry job for two years while laying the foundation for his entrepreneurial endeavor. During that time, he researched the local limousine market, prepared a detailed written business plan, added to his financial cushion and lined up his first customers – all while continuing to earn a steady income.

- *Start small and grow slowly*. The mistakes won't be as expensive that way, notes Art Koff of RetiredBrains.com. Nearly all of the featured business owners – even those who bought their own headquarter buildings eventually – had very modest beginnings in a garage, basement or some other area in their homes.

- *Find a mentor.* One place to look is SCORE, where you can get free mentoring – either face-to-face or virtual – from seasoned business people who volunteer their time to work one-on-one with aspiring entrepreneurs. Another way to cultivate mentors is through professional organizations or business groups such as the U.S. Chamber of Commerce.

- *Form an advisory board.* Like mentors, advisory board members can provide strategic thinking, a third-party perspective, solutions for unexpected problems and other help. With the right mix of advisors, you can obtain expertise in accounting, legal issues, marketing, human resources and other specific areas that can make, or break, your business.

- *Don't over-borrow, if you borrow at all.* This is a big one for many aspiring entrepreneurs. Just as credit allows you to get a house, a car and other big-ticket items you can't obtain otherwise, it can enable you to acquire office equipment and other necessities to launch a business. You also could find yourself over your head in debt if credit isn't managed carefully and kept to an affordable amount.

- *Find a partner who offsets your weaknesses.* "Entrepreneurs sometimes make the mistake of choosing founding partners who are like themselves, instead of bringing a diversity of strengths, talents and leadership styles, which make a more complete team," said Suzanne Magee. She described herself as "a risk taker" and "action oriented, with a big picture approach" while her business partner, Andrea Johnson, is more risk averse, thoughtful and pays attention to the details. "We are like yin and yang," Suzanne added, "and the balance we provide each other is essential."

- *Work for someone else first.* This approach may delay the dream of entrepreneurship, but it can be invaluable for people who want to open a business in an industry where they have no prior experience. Among other things, it allows you to make beginner's mistakes on someone else's dime and determine if the business is the right fit *before* you invest significant resources.

HAVE AN EXIT STRATEGY

Since you want to start a business, not get out of one, an exit strategy may not be on your radar – but it ought to be. Look at it this way: How you exit your business determines your ultimate success and profitability from the deal, so *not* planning an exit strategy increases your risk of things going wrong at the end.

In fact, you may need more than one exit strategy. Depending upon what you have in mind for your business, you could need several.

First, there's your strategy for when you decide to leave. Why you want to start a business in the first place could affect the method you choose to get out of it. For David Drewry, family involvement is key – which is why he opted to sell the home inspection business to his son and daughter-in-law after he and his wife, Anna, retired.

Cookies on Call's Franny Martin also has thought

about this question. "Ultimately, what I'd love to see happen is that I would stay involved but have a succession plan," she said. Her exit plan is different than it would have been if she had started her business in her 20s rather than her 50s. "What I would have done," said Franny, "is built a company to sell it."

What if your company doesn't meet expectations? At what point do you cut your losses? You may need an exit strategy to deal with that scenario as well.

Does your business idea call for diversifying into new products, or new industries, further down the road? Again, you'll need a plan to exit if the expansion doesn't work out.

For a 40-or-older entrepreneur, getting *out* of a company successfully requires as much planning and introspection as getting *in* – so expect to ask yourself more questions. Will you want to sell your business to family members or the next generation of managers? Would you like another company to acquire or merge with yours? Do you want to bow out completely and use your earnings to travel around the world? Or do you want to keep a toe in the water and stay part time? Even if you don't have all the answers right now, it's a good idea to start thinking about them.

MOVING FORWARD

All of the business people featured in this book took risks to move forward. Rory Kelly did when he left the steel business to become a limousine entrepreneur. David Drewry did when he left the military to go into the home inspection business. So did Donna Herrle when she introduced her graphic design firm.

Then there's Bonnie Alton, who made a dramatic career change when she went into the bakery business. For about eight years, Bonnie worked with a small business in the area of continuing legal education. Later, she became the director of marketing for a 300-partner law firm. After about a year, she realized she wasn't happy at the firm.

"I asked myself why it was such a bad fit," she said. "I was used to making a difference and having a valuable community." Neither was present in her work environment.

In 1994, she was talking about her professional situation to a friend, who mentioned that the owners of a new Great Harvest Bread Company franchise in Minneapolis were looking for a partner. Bonnie followed up on the lead, and one thing led to another. That year, she joined the bakery as an operating partner.

"While I was learning the business, I'd come in to the bakery at 4 a.m. or so and work for a few hours before going on to my day job," said Bonnie. "During that time, I was like a big sponge, soaking up as much information as I could." In 1998, when she was in her early 40s, she bought out the owners.

After 10 years at the same location, the bakery moved in 2004 when the rent became too high. Even though the new location is only 1.3 miles away from the old one, it was like starting over. That was also when the low-carbohydrate Atkins diet was in full swing. Sales in the fourth quarter of 2004 dropped between 15 and 16 percent compared to the same period one year earlier. Bonnie found herself having to do a lot of morale building among her staff.

"One day, two weeks after we opened in our new location, two things happened within 10 minutes of each other that I took as kind of a sign," she said. "One was two customers recognizing each other as old friends. The other was two people meeting up at the bakery for a discussion over a cup of coffee. After that, I knew everything was going to be okay.

"It took a couple of years to get through it all," continued Bonnie. "Now, we're economically poised, in part because rent is about half of what we were paying for the previous location." In 2010, the bakery was one of three to win Great Harvest's "Phenomenal Bread Award."

When asked what's behind her success, Bonnie pointed to her longing for community as well as her views about risk. "I recognized I had a certain tolerance for risk and I could apply that tolerance in a way that I could make a difference," she said.

To join the ranks of successful entrepreneurs, you'll have to take risks as well. That doesn't have to be a bad thing, however. Those of us who have been around for at least 40 years already know *anything* worth doing involves risks. Without them, there's no reward. As ice hockey great Wayne Gretzky said, "You'll always miss 100 percent of the shots you don't take."

The key is to *go out on the right limb.* Take the time to understand calculated risk, adopt the right perspective on luck and write a business plan. And while it may seem counterintuitive, start thinking about the end of your entrepreneurial endeavor now. Proper planning will save you a lot of grief – and help stack the deck in your favor.

NOW WHAT? 10 WAYS TO TAKE ACTION

1. Know what it means to take calculated risks. For key decisions, be prepared to weigh the possible results – both positive and negative – before moving forward. Research your business idea thoroughly so you can base your decisions on facts rather than assumptions.

2. Work for someone else first if you want to start a business in an industry where you have no experience. This lets you make beginner's mistakes on someone else's dime and determine if the business is a good fit before you invest significant resources.

3. Evaluate what you have to lose if your business fails. If the worst happens, can you live with the outcome? If the answer is no, don't start the business.

4. Talk with immediate family members. If you have a significant other and/or children, gauge their tolerance for the uncertainty that a business could create in their lives. Remember that you aren't the only one who's taking the risk!

5. Prepare a written business plan. It will force you to think through tough questions and address problems *before* they happen.

6. Find a mentor. Tap the experience of those who have been through the startup process already. Take advantage of the lessons they've learned to avoid making the same mistakes.

7. Form an advisory board. Recruit a diverse mix of members who have expertise or knowledge that you don't have, as well as a genuine desire to help you succeed. Look for people with strong problem-solving and strategic-thinking skills.

8. Start with adequate cash reserves. It should be enough to carry you through before you start making money. Consult with a financial advisor to determine how much you'll need.

9. Have a personal financial cushion that will be there regardless of what happens to the business.

10. Include an exit strategy in your business plan. If you envision the ending, it's more likely to happen the way you want.

CHAPTER 2
SWOT YOURSELF

Want to start a business that matches your strengths and interests? Then do what Tim Webb did. Get to know yourself better.

Before he switched careers in his late 40s, Tim worked as an attorney – a job he enjoyed. The issues were interesting, the people he worked with were smart and the compensation allowed him to lead a comfortable lifestyle.

He was good at what he did – maybe too good, because he reached a point where much of his client work wasn't challenging any longer. He felt restless and out of sorts – as if something were missing.

After 20 years of practicing law, Tim decided it was time to do something else. Yet he wasn't sure how to go about making a transition when he had been in the same career for so long. "As I thought it through, I figured the best way was to put myself through a self-assessment so I could identify and capitalize on my strengths," he said.

His assessment revealed that his strongest skills were writing and analyzing. That knowledge, combined with extensive research on different industries and preparations to get his finances in order, gave him the ammunition he needed to make a switch. At age 47, Tim left his law firm and moved to an international commercial real estate services company.

Once there, he joined a new business-development and brokerage team and voluntarily took on the job of dissecting and analyzing his new team's marketing proposals. As you can imagine, plowing through reams of paper wasn't a glamorous assignment. But he uncovered something that apparently had gone unnoticed before.

"I discovered that people on review committees read only the executive summary, introduction and conclusion of a proposal," he said. "It convinced me of the need to make the most important points upfront. Using the 80-20 principle, where you spend 80 percent of your time on the 20 percent that matters the most, I began spending most of the preparation time on the sections that were most likely to get read."

As they watched him throw himself into this initiative, Tim's colleagues realized that this was a guy who, despite his age, was willing to do whatever was needed, even when no one else wanted to do it.

In a short time period, the rate at which his team's proposals landed a presentation to a prospective client went from 20 percent to between 75 percent and 80 percent. Why? Because Tim had taken the time to assess himself professionally. He knew his strong suits – writing and analyzing – and applied them in ways that helped his new employer while elevating his personal success. He also knew that his colleagues, many of them 20 years younger, would be questioning if he had the tenacity to handle the demands of his new office, so he sought out assignments that proved he could.

Unlike the other people featured in this book, Tim Webb falls more into the category of "career changer" than "entrepreneur." But his story is here because it illustrates a principle that has relevance for late bloomers of *all* stripes.

You may be thinking about starting a business because, like Tim, you're burnt out on your current job. Or maybe it's because you've been laid off or want to be your own boss after years of working for someone else. Regardless of the reason, you're more likely to succeed if you follow an approach used by Tim and others who have transitioned from "safe, secure jobs" into new professional endeavors: Leverage your strengths and offset your weaknesses.

To do that, you have to know what your strengths and weaknesses are, of course.

THE ADVANTAGES OF A SWOT ANALYSIS

Most people who've spent decades in the workforce have had performance reviews ad nauseam, along with informal feedback in the form of compliments and complaints. You may be one of those people, in which case you have a handle on your professional capabilities already.

Still, some – or possibly many – of the skills, talents and traits that served you in the past aren't necessarily the ones you'll need going forward. Maybe, for example, your former bosses liked you because you never rocked the boat, but that tendency could work against you as a business owner. "Positives" can become "negatives," depending upon your new goals and the dynamics of your new business environment.

That's why you can benefit from a SWOT analysis, even if you think you know yourself well already. If you're unfamiliar with the term, SWOT stands for Strengths, Weaknesses, Opportunities and Threats. Companies use SWOT analyses to evaluate prospective businesses ventures, proposals and projects, but they also can be great tools for individuals. In your case, the "prospective business venture" to evaluate is whether you and your business idea have what it takes to succeed.

While a SWOT analysis isn't complicated, you can't rush through it. To do it right, you'll need to dedicate time to brainstorm and get input from people who know you well.

Once you get the hang of it, the SWOT technique can help you evaluate all kinds of opportunities and decisions related to your business. Thinking about bringing in a partner? Not sure whether to open a brick-and-mortar location to supplement your online presence? Use a SWOT analysis to guide you to the right answer. For a look at the basic process, see the "Conducting a SWOT analysis" worksheet at the end of this chapter.

When it comes to self-evaluation, those of us who are older have an advantage over younger business owners simply because we've been around longer. We've had more time to build a track record of successes and failures, work in different jobs, deal with a variety of clients and coworkers, and develop a management style. "I don't think most people really know themselves or their capabilities until they're in their mid-30s," said Tim Webb.

Among those who support the idea of a comprehensive self-assessment is Art Koff, who became an entrepreneur after nearly 40 years in advertising. During the last years in his former career, Art began researching the use of Internet marketing to reach older Americans, an unexplored area at the time. He found no existing websites, other than one hosted by AARP, that were directed at the seniors market.

As a senior himself, Art wasn't satisfied with his research findings. When he retired in 2003, he "didn't want to just play golf," as he put it. So instead, he created his own website and gave it a memorable name: RetiredBrains.com.

Early on, the site primarily offered links to places providing detailed information about Social Security, Medicare and other topics of interest to seniors. Later, it expanded to include a free job board to connect employers with older workers.

Today, Chicago-based RetiredBrains.com bills itself as "the premier destination for retirees, people planning their retirement and Americans caring for or having responsibility for older family members." Art, now 78 years old, remains actively involved with the site.

For him, what's especially rewarding is when RetiredBrains.com visitors express their thanks for the practical, easily understood information posted to the site. "I feel I am providing information to older

Americans which they can't find anywhere else," he said.

On a typical day, he receives around 200 emails from website visitors, including some who are exploring entrepreneurship. A few years ago, he wrote a book, *Invent Your Retirement: Resources for the Good Life*, used by some employers to counsel workers as they transition to retirement.

"I certainly feel research is necessary prior to starting a business, and part of that research should involve your own capabilities – your strengths and particularly your weaknesses – so you can find assistance in areas where you don't have experience or are weak," said Art.

Can you get by without a SWOT analysis? Most of the people interviewed for this book didn't do one – but when asked, just about all of them said they wished they had (or thought it was a good idea). Why not take advantage of this hindsight?

WHY PROFESSIONAL EXPERIENCE ISN'T ENOUGH

Most 40-and-over aspiring entrepreneurs assume their work experience gives them a big plus. They're right. In the Kauffman Foundation's 2009 survey of 549 company founders, 96 percent ranked prior industry/work experience as an important success factor for their most recent startup.[1] It certainly helped one of America's most famous midlife entrepreneurs: Sam Walton, who launched several Ben Franklin franchises before striking out on his own and opening his first Walmart in 1962 when he was 44.[2]

Still, work experience, by itself, isn't enough to make you a successful entrepreneur. Just because you're an accomplished computer programmer, writer, cook or whatever does *not* guarantee you have what it takes to run a business that offers those services.

What separates the business owners who succeed from the ones who don't? It has to do with "something extra" that goes way beyond work experience. The U.S. Small Business Administration says many successful entrepreneurs have these similarities:[3]

Persistence
Desire for immediate feedback
Inquisitiveness
Strong drive to achieve
High energy level
Goal-oriented behavior
Independent

Demanding

Self-confident

Calculated risk taker

Creative

Innovative

Vision

Commitment

Problem-solving skills

Tolerance for ambiguity

Strong integrity

Highly reliable

Personal initiative

Ability to consolidate resources

Strong management and organizational skills

Competitive

Change agent

Tolerance for failure

Desire to work hard

Luck

While you can't always count on your professional background as your ticket to entrepreneurial success, there's a flip side: If you possess a number of the traits from the list above, a lack of experience or formal professional credentials does not present an insurmountable obstacle for aspiring entrepreneurs. You may have to form an advisory board or partner with someone who *does* have the right technical expertise. You may even have to work for someone else in your new industry for a while. But you *do* have options to address this weakness.

Several people featured in this book faced this situation. They came from entirely different careers and/or had little or no technical training before founding their startups. Often, they had no formal business training, either. What they *did* have, however, was that "something extra."

One of these entrepreneurs is Annie Margulis, who founded a Michigan-based women's golf clothing company in 2005, when she was 48. With its bold colors and designs, Annie's clothing line – Girls Golf – attracts a varied clientele. Pros appreciate its style combined with functionality while non-golfers just like the look of its fashionable polo shirts, skorts, dresses, sweaters, Capris and accessories.

Annie's background isn't what you would expect for a golf-clothing entrepreneur. Before she started her company, she hadn't worked as a designer or a clothing buyer. For 25 years, she was a registered nurse at a Detroit-area hospital. She didn't even start playing golf until she was 38 years old!

Yet her strong work ethic and determination, two essential traits for successful entrepreneurship, were evident at a young age. By the time Annie was a junior in high school, she had enough credits to graduate. She also had a scholarship to nursing school – an opportunity that her parents, who didn't have much money, encouraged her to accept.

"Early on, my dream was to go into fashion," said Annie, "but it wasn't a practical choice at the time."

Over the years, Annie married and raised a family while working as a nurse. When she retired in 2000, her two children were almost grown – and she found herself wondering what to do next. A brief work stint at Saks Fifth Avenue rekindled her long-dormant interest in fashion. "I saw the store bring in all the clothing lines and just thought: I want my own business," she said.

As a golfer, the long-legged Annie had problems finding shorts that fit properly. She began working on a pair for herself, striving for a design that would appeal to other women golfers and could sell at fair price.

When her prototype was finished, Annie turned to Paul Dundas, a friend and an established women's clothing designer, who agreed to help. Soon, their collaboration yielded the first designs for the nascent clothing line. After they sold $15,000 worth of orders during their first trunk show (held in Annie's home in 2003), they never looked back.

Soon, the two partners began selling their colorful clothing at Lori Karbal, a local boutique owned by a friend. Annie also took the designs to a fashion industry show in Florida, where she handled all the logistics herself. "I didn't realize you were supposed to book appointments in advance," she recalled. "But a buyer from a major purchaser placed an order anyway."

A big break came when Annie sent a brochure, along with a brief handwritten note, to an editor at *Golf for Women*, then the world's top publication for female golfers. Within a couple of weeks, the now-defunct magazine requested samples (in size 2) of the entire Girls Golf line. It ended up featuring the clothes in several issues, providing national exposure for the brand. To keep up with demand, Annie and Paul moved most of their clothing production from a small, local facility in Michigan to a larger one in New York.

In 2005, Girls Golf expanded into Europe when Annie formed a partnership with Chris Endrich and Rike Vormwald. Today, Girls Golf has a presence in 200 locations throughout the U.S., Canada and Europe plus a few additional clubs and resorts in Dubai, South Korea and South America. Not bad for a one-time nurse who didn't design her first golfing shorts until she was in her 40s!

WHERE PASSION FITS IN

For Annie Margulis, Girls Golf is an ideal way to blend her passion for golf with her childhood dream of a fashion career. On that note, some may ask why "follow your passion" isn't one of the principles highlighted in this book. It's a fair question. After all, isn't "do what you love" a maxim for the most admirable business leaders?

In entrepreneurship, passion is very, very important. It gives you the dedication needed to keep going through the setbacks, rejection, long hours and all the other stuff that happens. But passion, like professional experience, isn't always a strength by itself. You also need *discipline* to make key business decisions based upon facts and data, rather than personal wants or likes.

Without discipline, entrepreneurs who buy and sell merchandise may fall victim to "the kid in the candy store" syndrome. People who turn a favorite hobby into a business may be especially prone to this tendency. Faced with a dazzling array of jewelry, handbags, rugs or other much-loved items, it becomes too easy to lose sight of what customers are buying and go hog wild with a wholesale order.

No one knows this better than my husband, Jim, a life-long cyclist who has two cross-country trips among his many two-wheeled excursions. Jim's passion led him to start a bicycle store, Spokes, Etc., in 1985. It also gave him perseverance during difficult times, such as a massive flood that ruined a warehouse of store inventory. Today, Spokes has five locations and is one of the largest specialty bicycle retailers in the country.

Like many athletes who are dedicated to their sport, Jim has personal preferences about the equipment he uses to ride. He also works as one of Spokes' buyers, a role that involves ordering millions of dollars each year in bicycles, components, clothing, accessories and other inventory.

Spokes uses the stores' sales history and trends to identify customer preferences, which in turn guide inventory-buying decisions. But suppose Jim allowed his personal preferences to dictate what he buys for his customers? If he orders 500 jackets in a style *he* loves – even though none of his customers bought or requested that style – the stores would have a big problem.

Before you list passion as a strength, evaluate whether you have sufficient discipline to balance your personal choices against the realities of the marketplace. Without discipline, your passion can become a major weakness, with the potential to undo your business.

FINDING YOUR WEAK SPOTS

While all of us like to hear positive things about ourselves, the not-so-fun part of a self-analysis is identifying weaknesses. We can't be good at everything, which means ability gaps are a fact of life for all business owners. Like Annie Margulis, who recruited a partner with the professional fashion design experience she needed, the best entrepreneurs acknowledge these gaps and find ways to offset them.

Take Franny Martin, who founded Cookies on Call, another Michigan-based company, when she was nearly 56. Franny had spent almost 30 years in corporate marketing, where she worked for some of the biggest names in business, including McDonald's Ray Kroc and Tom Monaghan of Domino's Pizza.

Franny decided to start her own cookie business when her father, a business owner himself, developed health problems. "I had spent my career in high-powered corporate-marketing positions," she said. "When my dad – who was my mentor and closest friend – became seriously ill, I went to see him.

I asked myself: 'If this were my last day on Earth, is this what I would want to be doing?' "

Having made up her mind, Franny moved quickly. She came up with the concept for her cookie company on a Friday and registered as a DBA (Doing Business As) the following Monday.

She began the company in her own kitchen, with friends and neighbors as her first customers. A turning point occurred when a food inspector suggested to Franny that she explore using a satellite kitchen. That recommendation led to an arrangement with a local elementary school to use its kitchen facilities, which gave her the space and equipment she needed to grow her business. After three years, she left the school and opened her own, commercial-grade kitchen

Today, Cookies on Call produces an average of 8,000 cookies each week and offers 48 varieties of cookies that it ships all over the world (the top seller: chocolate chunk). The company, whose revenue has increased each year since it opened, saw a 42 percent annual revenue increase in 2012. In addition to its online presence, Cookies on Call has two Michigan storefronts and plans to open two more. In 2013, it began selling a refrigerated, ready-to-bake product ("Fridge to Fabulous: Just Bake!") via local retail stores.

One key reason for Franny's growth is the way she allocated her time and focus. She did what she knew best – marketing – and hired others to handle the company's accounting, legal and technology needs, which weren't among her strengths. "You can't do everything yourself," she said. "To be successful, you have to be willing to say, 'I don't know.' "

Franny isn't the only one whose strong suits don't include technology. For older entrepreneurs, it's a common weakness, especially as it relates to social media. Unlike 20-and 30-somethings, who spend huge amounts of time online, they may not be proficient at sending tweets. They may use Facebook, LinkedIn and/or other social media outlets but have a limited understanding of how they work and/or their application in marketing.

John Olson, CEO of a pond and fountain supplies distributor, used to be in this category of entrepreneurs. John doesn't just dislike computers, he hates them. Still, he found a way to offset this weakness so effectively it put him ahead of his competition.

Prior to starting Graystone Industries, his Cleveland, Georgia-based company, John had a 15-year career with Publix Super Markets in Florida. As a store manager, he worked a regimented schedule where nights, weekends and holidays were the norm. In his spare time, he started a hobby: carving stone fountains and selling them to local nurseries.

Over time, the 60-and 70-hour workweeks took their toll. The final straw came when Publix underwent a restructuring that cut compensation for its managers dramatically. John took early retirement and spent six months thinking about what to do.

Meanwhile, his hobby flourished. As orders increased, and the piles of fountain parts grew higher inside his house, John realized he had to do something. "It was getting pretty cumbersome," he said.

In January 2005, just after his 40th birthday, John decided to incorporate – and Graystone Creations was born. Over time, other fountain makers began requesting supplies, so the company became a parts distributor (in addition to selling its fountains). It renamed itself Graystone Industries and, later, added pond supplies to its product mix.

As he built his business, John had to find a way around his aversion to computers, which he managed to avoid while at Publix. "I forced myself to learn one aspect," he said.

He picked Internet marketing, figuring it had the most value for what he wanted to do: Build his customer base. John taught himself about Search Engine Optimization (SEO) and other online marketing tactics, becoming so proficient that he wrote a book,

"The Pond Pro's Guide to....Internet Marketing," to help others in his industry.

John Olson's story shows how one entrepreneur managed to turn a weakness into an asset. Whether your weak areas include inexperience with the Web, a lack of familiarity with bookkeeping or difficulty managing third-party vendors, you need to identify them and take action. It's like a weight problem or a bad relationship: The sooner you face reality, the better off you'll be.

TO GET AHEAD, DON'T CUT CORNERS

In your eagerness to get going on your business, you may be tempted to skip the self-assessment. Don't. A SWOT analysis is effective and doesn't require complex or expensive computer software. You don't need much more than a piece of paper and something to write with.

If you prefer a more formal or professional approach to assessing your strengths and weaknesses, that's fine. Plenty of career coaches and consultants can help (for a fee, of course). The important thing is to go through the process somehow.

Remember, your objective is to identify strengths that you can leverage to create your own business. That's what David Drewry did when he started his home inspection business. "As a shop teacher, I had an understanding of mechanics and always had an interest in buildings," he said.

You're also looking to spot potential threats that, if left unaddressed, could derail you. That's something that happens all too often to entrepreneurs.

Consider what happened to Wally Amos, who created Famous Amos Cookie Company in 1975 when he was nearly 40. Ten years later, financial difficulties forced him to sell the company in pieces to outside investors. In a newspaper interview, Amos said he was the cause of the trouble, rather than any competitor. "I thought that I knew more than anybody else," he said. "I thought I was the main attraction, and I wasn't listening to other people."[4]

For some people, the SWOT analysis, or whatever form of self-assessment they choose, will unearth problems serious enough to warrant a change in direction. They may end up scrapping their business idea and going back to the drawing board. If that happens to you, it isn't the end of the world – as any serial entrepreneur will tell you. Be glad you found out now!

What if the outcome of your self-assessment discloses shortcomings that aren't automatic deal breakers but need attention? It may show, for example, that you have the people skills for your planned human resources consulting practice – but you're terrible at crunching numbers. Or that you're a wiz at marketing campaigns – a must for your proposed cosmetics company — but you aren't organized and can't keep track of paperwork.

Often, people who are in their 40s or older have been doing things a certain way for a long time. As a result, they're stuck in their ways and unreceptive to change. If that describes you, it presents a problem. Again, it's better you address that now.

On the other hand, you may be an aspiring entrepreneur who *is* open-minded and flexible. If so, you are more likely to find good solutions to shortcomings.

"We found experts when we were over our heads," said Sharon Dillard, who owns a franchise company in the kitchen-countertop and bathtub-resurfacing industry. "Leveraging the expertise of others is key to any successful business."

Like Sharon Dillard, Annie Margulis and Franny Martin, you can find trusted partners or consultants who possess critical expertise you lack. Like Tim Webb and John Olson, you can teach yourself new skills that you need to succeed.

The reality is that none of us can do it all. Even if you are 100 percent confident that your future company will produce the next hot fad, you're going to need help. So do yourself a big favor: *SWOT yourself.* Use it to find out where you stand. By addressing your weaknesses early, you free yourself to focus on your strengths – and apply them in ways to build a profitable business.

NOW WHAT? 10 WAYS TO TAKE ACTION

1. Do a SWOT analysis, even if you aren't the self-introspection type. To get started, review the "Conducting a SWOT analysis" worksheet at the end of this chapter.

2. Find out what makes you happy! The "strengths" section of your SWOT analysis will provide answers or clues.

3. Don't try to do a SWOT analysis in your head. Put it in writing. Get someone to help you if writing isn't your thing.

4. Choose reviewers who know you well and will give you candid feedback, rather than simply tell you what you want to hear.

5. Revise your business idea to incorporate strengths that will help you stand out from your competition. Example: If you plan to open a business as a writer, you could attract more customers if you possess – and

promote – an expertise in Search Engine Optimization.

6. Use the "strengths" from your self-analysis to write the section of your business plan that presents your credentials.

7. Go through each weakness and decide how you will offset it, whether it's by hiring the necessary talent or teaching yourself new skills.

8. Pay close attention to how you categorize your skills, knowledge and aptitude related to accounting, law and technology. These areas tend to be among the weakest for late bloomers. They also are among the most vital functions of businesses.

9. If you plan to work with a business partner, choose someone who will complement your strengths and fill in your "gaps." Don't base your decision on friendship or personality alone.

10. Analyze the strengths and weaknesses of your competitors and compare them with yours. Include the results in your written business plan.

CONDUCTING A SWOT ANALYSIS

The simplest way is to take a piece of paper and draw a box with four quadrants. Write the headings "strengths" and "opportunities" in the upper two quadrants and "weaknesses" and "opportunities" in the bottom two. Make a list in each. Be as specific as possible when choosing words/phrases.

Ask yourself these questions from the U.S. Small Business Administration:

> Are you a self-starter?
>
> How well do you get along with different personalities?
>
> How good are you at making decisions?
>
> Do you have the physical and emotional stamina to run a business?
>
> How well do you plan and organize?
>
> Is your drive strong enough?
>
> How will the business affect your family?

Here are other areas to consider:

> What's unique about you? What makes you stand out from the crowd?

What do you do better than anybody else?

What resources do you have that others don't?

What projects did you oversee that weren't successful?

What skills do you wish you had – but don't?

When were you glad to defer or delegate tasks to others?

In addition, think about:

Your tolerance for taking advice from someone younger than you

Whether you can adapt to changes that go along with working in a non-traditional office setting

Your money-management skills, including how you've managed credit in the past

When you're finished, share your list with people who know you well for their input. Choose people who will provide candid feedback, rather than simply telling what you want to hear.

CHAPTER 3
MAKE IT A FAMILY AFFAIR

One day, Grace Welch was changing her baby daughter's diaper as she talked with her sister about starting a business. Then something happened that changed Grace's life as well.

As she struggled to keep the baby from squirming off the changing pad, Grace snapped orders to her sister to bring wipes and other items. "What they need to do," she said in exasperation, "is get rid of this crazy pad."

That "aha" moment led Grace to create the Patemm pad, whose round design accommodates wriggling babies more easily than the rectangular shape of traditional diaper changing pads. Since Patemm's launch in 2004, Grace's family has influenced just about every key decision she's made while building her company.

With the exception of a few specialty brick-and-mortar stores that carry its products, Patemm operates online – a business model chosen by Grace and her husband/business partner, Marty, because it gives them more flexibility to organize their work schedules around the care of their four children.

In 2010, Patemm – which had been producing its products in San Francisco – moved east to be closer to its manufacturer in Massachusetts and to New York City, which Grace visits regularly to cultivate and maintain key media contacts. After considering several locations, Grace and Marty chose Providence, Rhode Island, as Patemm's new home because "it's family friendly," she said.

Even the company's branding reflects a family influence. The 28-inch Patemm pad derives its name from Grace's two oldest children, Patrick and Emma.

While they can't, or don't, always go to the same lengths as Grace Welch, most successful late-blooming entrepreneurs involve their families in their businesses. Rather than "this is my deal," these late bloomers see their entrepreneurial endeavors as package deals. *They make it a family affair*.

To some degree, they *have* to think this way. Family members or friends may be the only ones willing to provide the seed money needed to launch the business. With a shoestring budget, new entrepreneurs may have to rely on spouses/partners, children or other relatives, at least temporarily, to enter computer data, handle the bookkeeping, answer the phone, wait on tables or supply other labor needed to run the business.

On the flip side, household members have to accept and accommodate a new normal. For families who eat dinner together, that may mean changing their schedules or getting used to an empty chair at the table, at least for a while. If the startup operates out of the home, it may require physical adjustments, such as relinquishing garage space for inventory storage or turning a bedroom into an office.

There's more to the Make It a Family Affair principle than the practical aspects, however. For most of us, starting a business is the most difficult, risky – and thrilling – experience of our lives. It creates worries and stress that make for sleepless nights – as well as excitement and the potential for enormous personal, and financial, rewards.

Some business owners try to separate family from this emotional roller coaster – but for the most part, that doesn't characterize the late bloomers. Given the magnitude of entrepreneurship, they *want* to share it with those who matter the most – which is why they often partner with or employ family members. When immediate family members don't work directly for the business, they become cheerleaders and confidants. In these roles, they hear all about the setbacks and victories.

Out of all the principles in this book, Make It a Family Affair is one of the most critical. As you'll read in this chapter, family buy-in is key to entrepreneurial success. When a spouse, partner and/or kids go along for the journey and feel its twists and turns, they're more likely to "bond" with the business, which manifests itself in pride and support. As a result, your business will be better and stronger – and your personal life will be better and stronger, too.

FAMILY PRESSURES FACED BY LATE BLOOMERS

If you're over 40, chances are you have a life partner and/or dependents by now. But even if you don't, work/family balance is an issue that could affect the success of your entrepreneurial endeavor. As you build your business, you may bring in a partner, consultants and/or employees who *do* have families, so it helps to understand where these key members of your team are coming from.

At one time, the struggle to manage work and family demands may have been associated with younger professionals, but that's not the case anymore. A variety of factors, including a desire for career advancement and medical developments, has changed all that. Now, it's not at all unusual for couples in their 40s and beyond to marry or become parents for the first time, or add to their brood. Cookies on Call's Franny Martin didn't get married until she was 42. And look at former *Good Morning America* host Joan Lunden, who's now an entrepreneur. She had twins at age 54 through the help of a surrogate mother.[1]

Even if they don't have young kids, older entrepreneurs may be susceptible to family pressures for another reason: They've been around long enough to accumulate complex or extended-family situations. By the time they hit 40 or 50, they may have married, separated, divorced and/or been widowed (perhaps several times) and acquired stepchildren or other relatives along the way. They also may be caring for aging parents, making them members of the "sandwich generation." With so many dependents, these entrepreneurs *really* feel the effects when the demands of a new business compete with family responsibilities.

Just as it isn't limited to younger professionals, work/family balance isn't just a "women's issue" either. To the contrary, fathers in dual-income couples feel significantly greater work-life conflict than mothers, a study by the Work and Family Institute found. In 2008, 60 percent of the fathers in dual-income households reported work-life conflict versus 47 percent of the mothers. Compared with three decades ago, it's much more common and socially acceptable for men to help with the childcare, cooking, cleaning and/or other domestic responsibilities.[2]

And apparently, many men like it that way. The male entrepreneurs interviewed for this book seem to be as focused on family as the female ones. Tim Davis, a tech entrepreneur, is a good example. When asked about the principles he followed to build his consulting practice, Tim said he relied upon five "fs," as he called them. Four were "faith," "fitness," "friendship" and "finance" (income). Any guesses on the fifth?

While there's no universal list, here are some family pressures that aspiring late-blooming entrepreneurs may encounter (Chapter 7 looks at financial pressures more closely):

- Spouses and partners may balk at the idea of opening a business. Almost three-quarters of the company founders who participated in the Kauffman Foundation's 2009 research identified "family or financial pressures to keep a traditional, steady job" as possible barriers for potential entrepreneurs.[3]

- Both the entrepreneur and his/her significant other may worry about retirement money or health insurance. Fueling these concerns is the "time window" issue mentioned in Chapter 1 (if something happens to retirement funds, the window of time to replenish them isn't large for 40-and-older entrepreneurs).

- Late bloomers may have kids in college, which could mean huge tuition bills and other education-related costs on top of the expenses of starting a business.

- Over time, younger kids may become increasingly resentful if they rarely see an entrepreneurial parent. They can't count on him or her, especially during the early stages of entrepreneurship, to be in the audience for sporting events, performances or other special moments that matter to them.

- Vacations and other time away may not happen, causing disappointment for family members and stress buildup for the entrepreneur (who doesn't get a much-needed breather from the startup).

- Retirement-age spouses or partners who are ready to kick back and relax may resent it when the entrepreneur doesn't want to slow down as well.

HOW SUCCESSFUL ENTREPRENEURS MANAGE FAMILY PRESSURES

If these pressures weren't enough, entrepreneurs with families also face the same types of scheduling conflicts that cause anxiety for *any* working parent. Sometimes, there's no getting around the prospective client who wants to meet at the same time as a son or daughter's soccer tournament. Likewise, married entrepreneurs can't always prevent the out-of-town fundraising trip that falls in the same week as a wedding anniversary. Whichever party has to yield in these situations won't be too happy about it.

The people in this book aren't immune to these types of unavoidable scheduling conflicts or the family pressures outlined in the last section. But unlike some less successful business owners, they don't wait until family-related conflicts come knocking on their door before thinking about them. Rather than managing these conflicts on the fly, the best late bloomers try to anticipate them – and take steps *in advance* to work them into their new lives.

Sometimes this means forming business setups designed to achieve maximum work/family balance. Like Patemm's Grace Welch, they may choose a mostly online business format so they can work from home and have more flexibility to accommodate their kids' schedules.

Occasionally, they take their pro-family business setups to impressive levels. Graystone Industries' headquarters, a former executive retreat, is a multi-use facility that also serves as the family home of company CEO John Olson. It sits on a picturesque 7.5-acre site that has a golf course, fishpond and wooded trails. "I enjoy the lifestyle I have," he said. "The best part is I get to stay home with my family."

Aside from certain models or physical structures for their businesses, how else do entrepreneurs reduce the pressures that result when their business and family worlds collide? Here are a few ways:

FAMILY MEETINGS

Initially, family meetings are opportunities to outline the vision, present plans and discuss the support needed to move forward. Over time, they take on a different purpose. Regardless of whether they happen over a pizza or in a boardroom, these meetings provide *regular communication* about both progress and setbacks. Likewise, family members have an opportunity to voice any grievances and concerns, offering a way to address these issues *before* they turn into untenable problems.

HOME OFFICES

While it usually requires household adjustments, a home-based business can ease family pressures by freeing time (sometimes two or three hours) that otherwise would be spent commuting. It also eliminates the stress associated with traffic jams or crowded public transportation, which puts people in a better state of mind to deal with both work and family-related challenges. When your morning "commute" consists of a 30-foot walk down the hallway and the only "traffic obstruction" is the family dog, who wouldn't arrive at work in a good mood?

Bill Cheeks is among those who enjoy a home office arrangement. But as this financial-education entrepreneur notes, working from home isn't for everybody. "A lot of people can't because they don't have the discipline to do it," he said. Bill has his home office on an upstairs level separate from household noise and other distractions.

PROVIDING "SPACE"

Having family members as business partners can create too much togetherness, especially when they live together as well. One approach that seems to help is for each person to have separate, clearly defined areas of responsibility within the business. At Graystone Industries, the Georgia-based pond-supplies company, John Olson handles the marketing and customer service while his wife handles the accounting and programming functions. Grace Welch oversees public relations and marketing for Patemm while her husband is the office manager. Before they retired, David Drewry oversaw the inspections conducted by Drewry Home Inspections and his wife, Anna, managed the back-office function. With these types of partnerships, each spouse can do his or her thing without stepping on the other's toes.

LIFE PLANNING

In some cases, entrepreneurs balance business and family demands by not attempting to do everything at once. Some aspire to entrepreneurship early in their adult lives – when they may have little money, young kids, full-time jobs and/or a big mortgage. Rather than pursuing their dream then, they delay it until a more opportune time. Girls Golf's Annie Margulis, for example, waited until her children became adults before launching her clothing line.

TIME MANAGEMENT

For anyone hoping to run a business *and* uphold a commitment to family, one thing is clear: You can't do both well without time-management skills. Just ask Tim Davis, principal of Zalex, an Atlanta-based firm that offers Chief Information Officer (CIO) advisory and business-technology services to small and mid-sized companies. This includes interim CIO support for companies searching for a full-time CIO as well as fractional services for small companies that need help with their technology strategy.

Prior to Zalex, Tim was the CIO of Popeyes Louisiana Kitchen, where he oversaw the day-to-day operations of the restaurant chain's technology department. He enjoyed the work but grew tired of the demands and inflexibility of corporate life.

While Tim had dabbled in consulting since 2005, the real start of his company happened in 2008, after he won Georgia's CIO of the Year Award in the corporate category. "It got me thinking about what the future might hold for me," he said.

At the time, Tim was on the board of a local

technology magazine. When the publication asked him to do some work, he had his first client – and was off and running.

One aspect Tim enjoys most about having his own business is "working on fewer projects and going deeper with them." To create his consulting practice, he followed a simple approach. "I focused on something that I enjoy doing – and that I'm good at doing," he said.

He credits his years in the corporate world with getting him to where he is today. "I don't think I could have done this when I was younger," Tim said. "I didn't have the relationships and the network that I have now."

If Zalex weren't enough, Tim is involved with another startup he describes as "a social media site that intersects with politics." He belongs to several professional organizations and has a young family. Given his full schedule and the many items on his action list, effective time management is vital for Tim. In part, that means not waiting until the last minute to look at his calendar. Typically, he plans it two weeks in advance to ensure time for his priorities. At the top of this list is family: he tries to have a one-on-one breakfast or lunch with his wife and each of his two sons every week.

FAMILY BUY-IN

With the overwhelming number of decisions and action items needing attention during a startup's planning phase, some might ask if a family commitment, or "family buy-in," warrants a place among key preparations. The answer is no, it shouldn't be "among" them. It belongs at the top!

Why is family buy-in so critical? Without it, at least some, if not all, of the situations on the "family pressures" list *will* happen. Each of them has as much potential to doom a startup as a weak product idea, insufficient financing, a poor location, a faulty marketing strategy or other common culprits for business failures.

"A key question is whether there's a family commitment," said Patemm's Grace Welch. "If it's not there, how's that going to affect your business? You need to have that support system."

Clearly, Rory Kelly had the support of his family before starting Prestige Limousine. His wife, after all, gave him his first limo, a birthday present intended to serve as the starting point for a new business.

Donna Herrle, as mentioned earlier, didn't begin laying the groundwork for her graphic design company until she talked with her two sons. Recognizing that she might face insurmountable difficulties without their support, Donna wanted to make sure both sons were in her corner (which they were).

"My family was extremely affected," said Julie Savitt, the president and owner of a trucking company that hauls construction materials. When she assumed full ownership of the business, Julie was a single parent of three (not to mention a woman in a male-dominated industry). "We talked often about the need to be a team to survive," she said. "I would make goals for them. We had to keep going."

THE LATE BLOOMER'S FAMILY ADVANTAGE

While Julie Savitt faced many obstacles, she did have something going in her favor. She was among the many business owners in this book who came from families where at least one other member is, or was, an entrepreneur.

For these business owners, family buy-in comes more easily and here's why: to say their entrepreneurial relatives "understand" the demands, pressures and passion associated with a startup doesn't do them justice. They've *felt* these emotions down to their bones! They truly know what it's like to worry about meeting payroll or to deal with inventory headaches. With empathy comes a willingness to make the necessary sacrifices and a capacity to weather difficult and/or lean times.

Another business owner with entrepreneurial family roots is Barbara Cosgrove, who founded Barbara Cosgrove Lamps at age 47. Barbara, a trained artist, had an art studio for several years. By the time she reached her mid-40s, her two children were grown and the mortgage was paid. She was ready to do something else.

The problem was finding a suitable career, given her age, level of education and artistic nature. "If you're a creative person, you're only happy if you're doing something creative," she said.

"Looking back, there weren't a lot of options," added Barbara. "I had been making decisions all this time and wasn't going to have someone start making them for me."

In 1996, she started Barbara Cosgrove Lamps in her garage. For Barbara, the early days confirmed the importance of tenacity. "Someone said to me, 'This business is like a tiger. If you get off, it will eat you.' You have to figure out how to stay on."

Today, Barbara Cosgrove Lamps is an international lamp operation with 3,500 commercial clients. The Kansas City-based company, which had $2 million in revenue in 2012, has nine employees in its headquarters and 35 sales representatives nationwide.

For Barbara, one of the best things about being a business owner is the opportunity to exercise her artistic flair and creativity (she stays personally involved in every lamp design). She also enjoys the camaraderie and counts her competitors among her friends. "It's a very huggy, kissy industry," she said. "You spend many hours together at trade shows and get to know each other very well."

In 2007, *Country Living* magazine named Barbara as one of its top women entrepreneurs. She attributes her business acumen to listening to people, including her entrepreneurial husband. Her grandparents and father were entrepreneurs as well. "I've been surrounded by them all my life," said Barbara.

"Life experience brings a lot to the business table," she added. "By the time you're 45, you know certain things. You hear about the employee who steals and know not to hire people like that."

Patemm's Grace Welch also grew up in an entrepreneurial household. Before emigrating to the U.S. from the Philippines, her father and mother owned several businesses. "My parents' entrepreneurial spirit got into my blood," said Grace.

Beyond the family buy-in mentioned earlier, why does an entrepreneurial family history provide an advantage for Grace, Barbara and other business owners? They know that entrepreneurship isn't a pipe dream. Their spouses, parents or whoever started a business before them demonstrated that – with the right idea and good planning – it's very doable.

In addition, these entrepreneurs had witnessed and, to some degree, already lived the ups and downs of entrepreneurship by the time they started out on their own. Even though some had no formal business background or training, they had been through the school of hard knocks vicariously.

"Business is what we talked about at the dinner table," said Julie Savitt, whose parents and grandfather all were entrepreneurs. "Most people who grow up in it know the trials and tribulations," she said. "I think it's worth the risk."

Family exposure also taught these entrepreneurs about the enormous dedication and time commitment needed for successful business ownership. Cookies on Call's Franny Martin recalled how her father, also a business owner, gave her an item he had clipped from a magazine when she was in fifth grade. "Quitters Never Win and Winners Never Quit," it read. That early lesson served Franny well during a nearly 30-year career in corporate marketing – and remains her view as she operates her own company.

FIGURING OUT THE RIGHT ROLES

Just as some companies have anti-nepotism hiring rules, some employment specialists warn against entrepreneurial family members working together. It's easy to understand why.

When a relative doesn't pull his or her own weight, lacks key skills, or has other deficiencies that hurt the business, it can be painful to part ways. Who wants to be in the position of having to fire an underperforming son, niece, brother – or spouse?

And what about afterwards? An entrepreneurial rift with relatives creates a potentially awkward situation because you may not be able to avoid them forever. What happens when you bump into each other at a graduation party, or find yourselves seated at the same table for a wedding?

Fortunately, these problems don't seem to be typical for the late-blooming entrepreneurs in this book. To the contrary, most work well with family members and view them as valued, productive partners or team members. They admire the talents and skills these individuals have to offer. Lamp designer

Barbara Cosgrove, for example, said her daughter-in-law AJ, who handles Barbara's marketing, is "one of the best in the business."

Home inspector David Drewry has similar respect for his wife Anna. "She was a better deal-closer than me," he said. "It's good to balance each other's strengths and weaknesses."

Here's the other thing: These entrepreneurs *like* working with others in their family, an environment that can offer an unmatched level of trust and comfort. In addition, many want to "share the wealth" with family members and create a situation that allows all of them to prosper together.

"Family involvement turned out to be pretty key," said Richard Urban, a technology entrepreneur whose employees included two sons, a niece and a nephew. "They were very creative and committed – plus they grew a lot from the experience."

Entrepreneurs involve their families in all kinds of ways. When Annie Margulis began marketing the Girls Golf clothing line, her daughter was the model for a brochure featuring the outfits. That brochure, along with a brief handwritten note from Annie, caught the attention of an editor at *Golf for Women* – leading to multiple appearances in the magazine and national exposure for the Girls Golf brand.

Sometimes a spouse or partner is a co-owner, or

a grown child contributes professional skills as an employee or a consultant. One of Donna Herrle's subcontractors is her oldest son, who provides IT, back-office and other support ("We get along beautifully," she said).

In other cases, family members aren't involved with the business directly. Instead, they provide financial backing, advice, connections, referrals and/or emotional support that's critical for the entrepreneur's success. Cookies on Call's Franny Martin described her husband, Jim, as her "biggest cheerleader."

How do you figure out what level of family involvement will benefit your startup – and keep everyone on good terms? There isn't a one-size-fits-all approach. The right level depends upon several variables, ranging from the skills and interest of your family members to the personal chemistry you have with them.

More often than not, people don't think about this question upfront, in part because they're focused on other things and assume the family stuff will work itself out. The compatibility of management styles and work habits – as well as tolerance levels for pet peeves – may not come up until later (when it's too late).

If you and your spouse/partner, or another

family member, are thinking about working together, you're better off not "winging it." Make it part of your pre-launch research to find out what works best for you.

DON'T TRAVEL THE ROAD ALONE

Sure, you can find entrepreneurs who started a business while leaving their families out of it. But if they had success, it probably wasn't sustainable. Or it came at a high cost, either professionally or personally (or both).

The inclusion of family members isn't a panacea for the pressures associated with starting a business. Sometimes the stress, worry or financial burden destroys the business or a marriage (or both), even when the non-entrepreneurial spouse or partner is fully engaged. At least one interviewed entrepreneur became divorced after starting a business.

Still, the success enjoyed by the people in this book shows the Make It a Family Affair principle is worth adopting, in some way. Maybe that means direct involvement – or maybe it doesn't.

In my case, an indirect, support-from-the-sidelines approach works well. While he isn't a writer or a communications consultant (and has zero interest in becoming either), my husband, Jim, has helped me avoid mistakes that could have turned into disasters. Those of us who have been in a relationship for a long time trust our spouses' or partners' judgment and find value in their views and opinions, even if they aren't fully knowledgeable about our business.

After a SWOT analysis or other research, you may go this route as well and decide that you're better off involving family members indirectly – as confidants, cheerleaders or investors, rather than business partners or employees. That's fine. Just involve them somehow and *make it a family affair.*

By taking them along for the journey and adopting some of the techniques outlined in this chapter, you'll be better positioned to maneuver the rough patches in the road ahead. It won't be easy. Your spouse, partner and/or kids will feel the pressures, conflicts, hassles, disruptions and inconvenience. But they'll also experience the victories and be more likely to provide the buy-in and commitment you need.

In entrepreneurship, ups and downs are part of the game – a game that becomes so much more satisfying and enjoyable when we play it with those we love. The way to success requires adopting a family philosophy of "we're all in this together."

NOW WHAT? 10 WAYS TO TAKE ACTION

1. Meet with your spouse/partner and reach a mutually acceptable agreement *before* you begin work on the startup. Without this buy-in, your business idea – or your relationship – won't succeed.

2. Hold an initial meeting with all immediate family members to present the business idea. Be realistic about time, money and personal sacrifices. Emphasize the importance of a family commitment. Let everyone ask questions.

3. If you plan to run the business from your house, get input from family members on how to minimize the disruption that will come from sacrificing a room, garage or other space.

4. Define your family network. Do research on cousins, in-laws and other relatives you may not know well. Who does what? What kind of professional support can they provide?

5. Recruit teenage or college-age relatives to provide social media assistance if you aren't knowledgeable in this area.

6. Focus only on family members who would be assets to the business. Rule out any who, for whatever reason, might be destructive.

7. Enlist entrepreneurial family members to serve as advisors. Take full advantage of their experience and knowledge as long as they're willing to be supportive (see No. 6).

8. Identify available resources and behind-the-scenes support needed to launch the business. Can relatives provide financial backing or childcare during business trips?

9. Hire your children when they're old enough to work after school, in the summer or over school breaks. The experience will give them a better understanding and a deeper connection to your business, even if they decide to pursue a different career once they are out on their own.

10. Keep family members in the loop through regular conversations and/or meetings. Don't hide bad news they need to hear. At the same time, let them know when you've reached milestones, so they can celebrate with you.

CHAPTER 4
KNOW WHO YOU NEED TO KNOW

It's not what you know, it's who you know. Think about that adage as it relates to your own life.

When you graduated from school, did you use your contacts – or those of a parent – to land your first "real" job? If you did, you weren't alone. Most people in their late teens or early 20s need help getting a foot in the door, since they don't have much work experience.

As you climbed the corporate ladder, did you reach out to people who were in a position to put in a good word for you? When you were the one doing the hiring, did you ask around for recommendations, so you didn't have to wade through hundreds of résumés?

Like it or not, "who you know" matters. In a perfect world, consultants and vendors would compete for new business based upon qualifications – and nothing else. If the selection-committee chair happened to be friends with the marketing director of a competing firm, it wouldn't tip the decision-making process. The world doesn't work that way, however.

Some industries exist because of relationships. Typically, the executives at lobbying and public relations firms are former legislators, regulators or journalists, or they had other key roles related to public policy. As a result, they have an insider's knowledge of the legislative or media relations process and can navigate these systems on their clients' behalf. They also know people in office who have influence in policymaking areas that matter to their clients.

For a new business, the right connections – or lack of them – can mean everything. Whether a startup obtains certain product lines, negotiates affordable supplier rates, recruits qualified employees, bids on certain projects, reaches key markets – or achieves just about *any* goal – often depends upon its relationships.

Almost all of the entrepreneurs interviewed for this book networked, either consciously or subconsciously, to start and grow their businesses. In the Kauffman Foundation's 2009 survey of 549 company founders, 73 percent ranked professional networks as important to the success of their business. Sixty-two percent of the survey respondents felt the same about personal networks.[1]

To succeed at entrepreneurship, you will need to network as well. That shouldn't be a major revelation since, in one way or another, you've been networking all your life. What's changed is your role: For you, the question now becomes "What relationships do I, *as an aspiring or new business owner*, need to succeed?" Having an awareness of how established entrepreneurs apply their networks, as well as their views on connecting with others, can help answer that question.

HOW ENTREPRENEURS NETWORK: TWO CONTRASTING STYLES

For a few late-blooming entrepreneurs, networking isn't intentional or premeditated. When they begin laying the groundwork for their startups, "build a network" doesn't enter their thought process as a necessary step. For them, networking is a byproduct of their efforts to build their businesses. As needs arise, they reach out to others.

Take Graystone Industries' John Olson, for example, the one-time grocery store executive who turned his fountain-making hobby into a pond-supplies business. "I'm kind of a lone wolf," said John. "I tend to find people I need via the Internet, rather than through [traditional] networking."

Michael Penny, an entrepreneur who started an organic mattress company, also leaned toward the non-intentional approach in the early days of his business. "I did have a network but, in hindsight, I do not think it was strong enough," said Michael. "It helps if you have someone who can give you feedback and when you have enough people to call upon."

Entrepreneurs like Michael and John seem to be in the minority. For most of the interviewed business owners, networking is a deliberate, proactive activity. They attend conferences, play golf, join organizations and visit social media sites to meet people who may become useful business contacts.

Like Drawing Conclusions' Donna Herrle, they see networking as critical for forming the relationships needed to create, launch and grow their businesses. Donna joined five networking groups and, whenever possible, found out in advance who would be attending the meetings. From her research, she culled a list of people to meet at each event – an approach that led to new clients. "Networking was my lifeblood at the beginning," she said.

Another avid networker is Suzanne Magee, president and CEO of TechGuard Security, a multi-million-dollar cybersecurity company she cofounded in St. Louis, Missouri at age 46. For aspiring entrepreneurs who dream about starting a business in a different industry, Suzanne's story demonstrates that such a leap is possible.

Suzanne isn't a programmer or some other type of technician associated with computer security. Astonishingly, she began her professional life as a flight attendant. It was a position that took her to new places literally and figuratively.

In 1979, she parlayed the contacts and knowledge acquired from her job to launch her first entrepreneurial endeavor: Flightgear, a mail-order company that sold luggage and other items for airline travelers. Along the way, she learned fundamental business operations, from filing quarterly taxes to processing credit-card payments. "That experience helped me tremendously," she said. "It showed me that it's possible to start a business."

By 1998, she was the director of business development for a computer startup. That year, President Clinton announced Presidential Decision Directive 63, which called for "a closely coordinated effort of both the government and private sector" to protect the nation's computer infrastructure, deemed critical for national security and economic operations.[2] The president's call for action resonated with Suzanne.

"I saw this as a mission that needed to be addressed," she said.

When she broached a recommendation to expand into the security field, her employer wasn't interested. She left her job, with a vision of starting her own computer-security company.

"I had this idea but I wasn't sure how to get there," Suzanne said. That changed after she accepted an invitation to an event held by the National Association of Women Business Owners (NAWBO), where she met many highly accomplished women.

Inspired, she joined NAWBO, became an active participant and made new contacts. Among them were an attorney and other professionals with expertise in areas of importance to startups. "I used those contacts to get answers and go where I needed to go," she said.

In February 2000, Suzanne and her business partner, Andrea Johnson, began TechGuard Security in the basement of Suzanne's home. The company had no revenue its first year. Then the terrorist attacks of September 11, 2001 happened, prompting Suzanne to secure a Small Business Administration loan that enabled TechGuard Security to weather the post-tragedy recovery. By its fourth year, TechGuard Security's annual revenue reached $1 million.

A major reason for TechGuard Security's growth is its entry into government contracting – another networking offshoot. The firm benefited from its longstanding participation in a breakfast series intended to introduce St. Louis-area companies and government agencies to one another. In 2004, Suzanne relocated TechGuard Security's head-quarters from St. Louis (where it still maintains an office) to the Baltimore, Maryland area, to be closer to federal government clients.

One of TechGuard's primary products is PoliWall, a security device that allows system administrators to block high-risk Internet addresses from a particular country with a click on a world map. In 2012, the company formed a subsidiary, Bandura, to market its PoliWall technology internationally. TechGuard Security is on track to gross over $10 million in 2013, said Suzanne.

Another "active networker" is Bill Cheeks, owner and president of ABBA Associates, a Powder Springs, Georgia-based firm that provides fis-cal-management consulting services for companies, government agencies, nonprofits and individuals. He's a popular speaker who conducts seminars nationwide to educate consumers and small busi-ness owners about credit and money management.

Bill loves being the owner of a business that lets

him travel and meet new people regularly. "For me, networking comes naturally," he said.

Since he works from home, Bill doesn't have to sit in rush-hour traffic or deal with other headaches associated with commuting. He sets his own schedule and takes on projects because he *wants* to, not because he *has* to. On top of it all, he earns more money now than when he was working for someone else.

Prior to starting his business in 2002 at age 57, Bill spent 34 years with Equifax, Inc., one the country's three major credit bureaus. During his last years with Equifax, Bill's networking skills helped him lay a foundation for his next professional endeavor.

Recognizing he would need administrative support, he cultivated contacts who could provide those services once he was out of the corporate world. He also participated in Equifax's loaned executive program, which assigned him to an organization that later became one of his first clients.

Today, Bill augments his network by staying involved in a long list of community organizations, including United Way, Boys & Girls Clubs of America, Operation Hope and the Jump$tart Coalition for Personal Financial Literacy. Volunteering, he points out, is a great way to network.

"I tell people: Volunteer for a charity because the

people who volunteer are high-level executives," he said. "That way, they get to know you in a different environment."

He has a LinkedIn presence and sends emails once or twice a week to many of his key contacts. "Once you meet me, I make sure I stay in touch with you," said Bill.

DON'T JUST NETWORK.
PAY IT FORWARD.

If you adopt an active, deliberate style of networking, will that be enough to find and build the relationships you'll need as a business owner? Actually, no. Most of the late bloomers in this book also abide by another networking mantra: Be willing to help others.

Bob Littell, principal of Littell Consulting Services, has a concept he calls "NetWeaving." It's a "golden rule" or "pay it forward" type of networking where people focus on putting others' needs first.

Here's how it works: You have two contacts who you think would benefit from meeting each other. Through a virtual or some other type of introduction, you help them exchange bios and arrange to meet in person. When the two parties get together, synergy occurs (hopefully) and a new partnership may form, or they find other ways to help each other. After the meeting, they follow up with you, so you know the outcome.

"People tell me all the time they've been doing this type of connecting for years," said Bob. "They just never knew what to call it before."

So how does the strategic matchmaker, or "NetWeaver," benefit from connecting others? Part of the reward is the "rush" that comes from facilitating a new business relationship that leads to exciting (and sometimes life changing) results. In addition, the premise behind NetWeaving is "what goes around, comes around," meaning the people you connect might return the favor one day.

The success of Bob's approach depends upon participants avoiding three mistakes. "One is when you call it NetWeaving but what you're really doing is networking," he said. "Another is failing to recognize 'takers' and permitting them to use you."

The third is "forgetting who brought you to the dance," meaning the two parties don't follow up with the person who connected them. If that happens, the NetWeaver should take the initiative to see how the connection turned out.

Aspiring entrepreneurs tend to like NetWeaving because it's about helping others and lacks the superficiality of traditional networking. "People often leave corporate life to get away from office politics," Bob pointed out.

For NetWeavers, a business dependent upon relationships means much more than making new contacts and staying in touch with old ones. It means understanding people's needs, keeping them informed and helping them form partnerships with one another to achieve mutual or complimentary goals. Those basic tenets form the backbone of NetWeaving.

The reality is that some traditional networking is necessary for aspiring and established business owners. Sometimes you just want quick answers, or you encounter people who are willing to help you in the short term – but that's it. NetWeaving, however, can be a more comfortable, effective way to establish lasting relationships. Usually, those connections turn out to be the most instrumental for achieving strategic objectives.

USING NETWORKS FOR EVERYDAY PURPOSES

In addition to attaining long-range business goals, late bloomers use their networks for a variety of practical, day-to-day purposes. Among them:

REFERRALS

During the interviews for this book, the use of networking for referrals or recommendations came up repeatedly. Just about all business owners, regardless of whether they have a franchise, an independent storefront or an online service, network to find consultants, employees, suppliers and others who will play a key role in their operations. Even when entrepreneurs rely upon websites and other online resources to research prospects, they usually supplement this effort with networking – i.e., asking people they know and/or respect if they've worked with the person or company under consideration.

Why do so many entrepreneurs tap their networks for referrals? In a word: trust. To find the right consultant – someone who has a good reputation, solid experience and fair prices – a trusted contact may provide the best avenue. The reverse also is true – referrals lessen the odds of hiring the *wrong* business partners, a mistake that can be disastrous. "The help you get from networking to find [needed expertise] usually saves a great deal of money if it comes from reliable sources," said Art Koff of RetiredBrains.com.

In addition, entrepreneurs may use their networks for cooperative referrals. If they're overbooked or don't offer a particular service, they'll recommend another credible service provider – who may return the favor one day. Prestige Limousine's Rory Kelly, who serves as a backup for other limo services in the same market, uses his network this way. It's an approach that depends upon "developing relationships of trust, availability and dependability," he said. "My core companies know I am not going to steal any of their clients."

PRODUCT TESTING

Focus groups, surveys and other types of market research can cost thousands of dollars – an expenditure that's out of the question for most startups. A more affordable alternative is to ask family, friends, former work colleagues, neighbors and other contacts to provide feedback on a product or service while it's in development.

One entrepreneur who did this is Grace Welch, founder of Patemm. Initially, Grace distributed changing pad samples to other mothers she knew, as well as to mothers she met during visits to the park with her children. The feedback helped her refine her product and begin building a market.

"If a mom loves a product, she's going to tell another mom," Grace said. More often than not, that communication occurs online, she added, as mothers make up a viral community that's "very, very strong."

Entrepreneurs may use their networks to test other facets of their business that can make or break its success. Franny Martin, the founder of Cookies on Call, knew that the delivery of her products would influence her customer's perceptions, so she used her contacts to test different carriers. "I would send a dozen cookies to each of their homes with a long questionnaire that asked about the speed of the delivery and the condition of the cookies when they arrived," she said. "Based upon this feedback, I was able to determine which carrier I wanted to use."

Technical Knowledge

Entrepreneurs have to deal with a whole array of administrative and operational questions, an area they may have glossed over when they thought about starting a business. Among these questions: What to do about billing, payroll, taxes, computer systems and customer data collection, to name a few examples.

And what about the entrepreneur who has a startup in an unfamiliar industry? If you're opening a restaurant after a 30-year career as an aerospace engineer, another category of technical information comes into play. Even with a partner who has experience in the new industry, the business owner faces the sometimes overwhelming task of getting up to speed on suppliers, product lines, customer trends, operating requirements and restrictions, and a host of other industry-specific areas.

Community college classes, seminars, books, trade publications and the Internet offer ways for entrepreneurs to educate themselves on technical topics. Chances are that you can go to a video-sharing website like YouTube and find a "how to" video on whatever process you need to know. Still, none of these options compares with talking one-on-one with someone who's *lived* that experience and can answer specific questions. A network can be a great place to get technical information and advice from people who have "been there."

MARKETING AND PUBLIC RELATIONS

Some of the interviewed entrepreneurs formed an initial e-marketing database by compiling email addresses from their current contacts. This approach provides two big advantages: You already have the addresses, plus it's much easier to cultivate customers among people who know you already.

Over time, entrepreneurs add new contacts to this database, positioning it to become a customer retention tool. Often, seasoned entrepreneurs, like ABBA Associates' Bill Cheeks, say they prefer communicating with their customers via email or texting, which provides convenience and speed yet allows for a more personal touch than many social media outlets.

Entrepreneurs whose previous jobs involved public relations know how to combine this skill with networking to cultivate media contacts. This, in turn, enables them to obtain media exposure that helps sell products or services. Prior to starting her company, Grace Welch managed the public relations, marketing and branding efforts for an architectural firm. Over the years, she used that expertise to obtain exposure for her Patemm pads on *The Oprah Winfrey Show* and *The Big Idea with Donny Deutsch,* in addition to numerous print and online publications. Recognizing the marketing value of that publicity, Grace visits New York City often to maintain key media contacts and develop new ones.

RetiredBrains' Art Koff combines media relations with networking by following personal-finance columnists and reporters who write about retirement issues. Whenever he sees an item of interest or relevance to his area of expertise, he contacts the reporter to let him or her know about RetiredBrains. com and the type of information it can provide. Through this approach, Art has built a network of media contacts that reach out to him – which in turn, gets his website in the news regularly.

WHOM SHOULD YOU INCLUDE IN YOUR NETWORK?

With a sense of how established business owners use their networks, you can build your own with the same objectives in mind. In addition, you can apply the same rules of thumb they use to decide whom to reach out to for maximum benefit.

"You don't want 'yes men' surrounding you. Your core of friends needs to be honest," said Cookies on Call's Franny Martin. In other words, the most valuable contributors will be people who tell it like it is, even if it's painful to hear.

"Find people who are smarter than you," said Patemm's Grace Welch. For late bloomers, here's another reality: The people smarter than you often are younger as well, especially in the realm of technology.

Aside from smart, candid people, who specifically

should be part of your network? Here's what established business owners suggest:

MENTORS

Sometimes the best mentor is a competitor (provided the two of you aren't in the same immediate marketplace) because he or she knows your industry as well as your business challenges. Mentors from other industries also can be valuable, as they provide a perspective that's outside your usual world.

Business groups, such as the Chamber of Commerce, SCORE or professional associations, are ideal places to meet potential mentors. When David Drewry was just beginning his home inspection business, he came across a website for the American Society of Home Inspectors (ASHI) and registered for one of its training conferences. "I asked myself how I could get the most out this conference," said David. "The answer was to buy as many drinks as I could to pick the brain of the other participants."

That turned out to be a smart move. David left the conference with several new contacts, including a few who became instrumental to his success. It also marked the start of his association with ASHI, for which he served as a board member and founded its Northern Virginia chapter.

SUPERSTARS

Business leaders who have "made it" can inspire you to reach heights you wouldn't achieve on your own. Tim Webb, the attorney who switched to commercial real estate, recommends "cultivating a relationship with superstars." He isn't referring to household names in the entertainment business, of course. He's talking about individuals within your industry who have achieved the level and type of success you want to achieve.

Tim believes a good place to find superstars is through trade journals, which typically feature stories about established industry leaders. The next time you read one of these articles, why not email or hand-write a note to the profiled person? Your message could mention a specific challenge or two you may be facing in your own business, along with any related points in the article that you found especially helpful. The superstar will appreciate your note – and may even reply. Who knows – it could lead to an important connection.

That raises another point about cultivating relationships with leaders. Usually, people reach superstar status within their industries because they're exceptionally good at what they do. Often, that puts them in a position to know good work or talent when they see it – and perhaps to back a deserving newcomer.

"We knew the major players and had some personal credibility with them," said tech entrepreneur Richard Urban, whose products helped detect payment-card fraud. "Without their support, it would have been a very tough sell."

TECHNICIANS

You never know when a team member will get sick, quit, move or have another situation that prevents him or her from working with you – so it's a good idea to know third parties who have the technical skills needed to step in if necessary. For entrepreneurs, legal and accounting experts are especially useful contacts to cultivate, Other key, third-party areas are website development, computer technology and distribution systems. If your current network includes multiple people with expertise in these areas, and they're people you trust and like, you're ahead of the game.

For aspiring entrepreneurs, one of the attractive features of franchises is they come with an instant network of technicians. Great Harvest Bread Company, for example, supports new franchise owners by providing them with access to specialists in training and development, site selection and other areas of business management. This support doesn't negate the need for networking, however. Franchise owners stand a better chance of success when they're well connected within their local communities.

CHEERLEADERS

"Cheerleaders" help you dust yourself off when you fall (which you will). They know how to give you a pep talk to restart motivation. They might be the industry superstars you cultivate, as well as former bosses, coworkers and others with whom you have a professional relationship. They also can be family members and friends – and should include significant others, of course. Having people who will be there for you – no matter what – is crucial!

DEVIL'S ADVOCATES

These people will find the problems or the side of the story you didn't think about. "Devil's advocates" look at things from all angles. They often lead in with, "What about…." or "Have you thought about…." In the eyes of some, they come across as naysayers or wet blankets. Why would you want to include them in your network? They tend to be right! Listening to them can save a lot of grief down the road.

SOCIAL MEDIA VERSUS IN-PERSON CONTACTS

If the goal is to have a network that helps achieve short-and long-term objectives related to starting a business, which is better – in-person or social media contacts? The answer: you need both, even if you're still figuring out the latter.

As mentioned before, technology is a common weakness for older entrepreneurs. They tend to prefer a face-to-face approach to networking, where they go to events and shake hands with people. When they have personal Facebook and Twitter accounts, the contacts tend to be the same ones they interact with in person – unlike their children whose several hundred Facebook "friends" typically include people they barely know.

Many of those interviewed said they have limited use of social media, at least for now. "It's sort of lame," said one. "I don't really understand it," confessed another. "It's a generational thing."

Along with this lack of understanding comes a fear of making a mistake that results in unexpected exposure in cyberspace. One entrepreneur said this happened to him after he accepted an invitation to join an acquaintance's network on LinkedIn, a business-focused social media outlet where professionals can "connect" and join groups related to their field. Unbeknownst to him, the acceptance of the invitation triggered a message to all his email contacts, inviting them to join *his* LinkedIn network (which he didn't know had been set up for him). The experience was a bit unnerving for him, but it also had a positive side. "I ended up getting a couple of new assignments," he said with a laugh.

While they may be leery, late-blooming entrepreneurs recognize that social media is here to stay – so they are taking steps to understand it better in the context of both personal networking and customer outreach. Some entrepreneurs like Savvy Rest's Michael Penny hired younger people with technology aptitude to set up and maintain a social media presence and provide advice.

Several entrepreneurs interviewed for this book waded into the social media scene by creating a LinkedIn presence that's intentional (unlike the example just given). For the uninitiated, LinkedIn has a help center and offers free learning webinars that explain the basics. As they become more comfortable, LinkedIn users can join professional groups that allow them to network with others in their field.

Like other areas of technology, social media evolves constantly. By the time you read this, more networking platforms will be out there or waiting in the wings. One way or another, they'll affect how you network, so pay attention to what's going on.

THE GOOD NEWS

As this chapter pointed out at the beginning, professional advancement depends upon networking. It's how people learn about jobs, get promotions and find other key opportunities – as anyone who's lived on this planet for at least 40 years knows.

Now that you're about to start a business, "who you know" becomes more important than ever. So ask yourself this: How much time and effort did you dedicate over the years towards building and maintaining your professional network?

Maybe you answered "not much" because, until now, you've buried yourself in your day-to-day responsibilities and rarely got away from your desk. Maybe you didn't join professional organizations – or if you did, you weren't an active participant (which is the only way you *really* get to know other people). If any of those scenarios sounds familiar, you've got some work to do.

On the other hand, you might be someone who *did* take advantage of opportunities to form relationships through various jobs, organizations and activities. If that's the case, you are in far better shape. But you're not off the hook, either.

Sure, some of your existing contacts will be very valuable – especially if you're staying in the same industry for your new business. "Though your peer group is likely to change, you can still build your network using contacts from your former business life," said Designing Conclusions' Donna Herrle.

But as you've read in these pages, your network also should include "superstars" and other business people who have made it big in your line of work. Even if you're used to networking, the thought of reaching out to people at this level may be daunting. Typically, they operate in powerful business and social circles, and are extremely busy. Why would they bother to take your call or respond to your email?

That brings us to the good news.

"Entrepreneurs want to give back," said TechGuard Security's Suzanne Magee, a prime example. While running a multi-million-dollar company, she's been giving back for years through her volunteer work and mentoring efforts.

So have many of the other entrepreneurs in this book, as well as many of the best-known business owners in America. They have a genuine desire to help others, especially aspiring entrepreneurs, for several reasons.

For one thing, they want to foster entrepreneurship and everything it represents – independence, freedom, unlimited potential and the pursuit of the great American dream. Graystone Industries' John Olson, for example, says one of his goals "is to help others prosper and enjoy the type of lifestyle I have."

In addition, the entrepreneurs you admire were in your shoes once. They want to provide encouragement – just as someone did for them when they were getting their business off the ground.

Look at it this way: You possess ambition, desire and vision – and you're asking for advice because you admire what the business owner has achieved. Who wouldn't respond positively to that type of outreach?

When asked what advice they would give to someone who's over 40 and wants to start a business, the most common response can be summed in two words: *Reach out.*

"I utilized contacts extending back to my first jobs in business," said Franny Martin of Cookies on Call. "It's amazing how willing people are to extend you a hand."

If you take the initiative and reach out, you're likely to be rewarded – as long as you remember this: Networking is a two-way street. Sure, you're contacting established entrepreneurs and others with expertise related to startups because you need help. It shouldn't be all about you, however. Be willing and prepared to offer help in return.

Networking is a constant process, or at least it should be. As your business evolves, so will the expertise you need. Expect to devote time to augmenting your network, as well as renewing some of your old acquaintances.

The bottom line is that an effective network is essential to your entrepreneurial success. But remember: The effectiveness of your network isn't measured by size alone. Don't get caught up in the tendency to measure how you're doing by the number of names in your address book. Focus as much on quality as quantity. *Know who you need to know.*

Finding the right mentors, technicians, superstars, devil's advocates and others who can help your business reach its potential will take time, work and dedication – but it will be worth the effort. Along the way, you'll meet fascinating, inspirational people – and form relationships that last a lifetime. It could end up as one of the most enjoyable parts of the startup process.

NOW WHAT? 10 WAYS TO TAKE ACTION

1. Make a list of who you know. Who's in your personal network right now?

2. Assess your contacts. Which ones are mentors, superstars, technicians, cheerleaders or devil's advocates? See who falls within these categories – and where you have holes.

3. Do research to "know who you need to know" to be successful in your chosen business. Read trade journals and blogs regularly to learn about the superstars in your business/industry.

4. Use a combination of in-person and social media outreach to build your network. If you don't understand social media, learn from someone who does.

5. Join and use LinkedIn. Register for one of its free webinars to learn how to get the most out of your account.

6. Volunteer in ways that allow you to give back to the community yet also introduce you to business people who may be useful additions to your network

7. Understand the difference between networking and NetWeaving. Know which one you're using when you reach out to people.

8. Cultivate a genuine desire to help others – then look for ways to do so regularly.

9. Remember that networking is a constant process. Dedicate time each week towards maintaining and adding relationships.

10. Follow through! If you tell a contact you'll do something, do it! It's amazing how many people fail to take this step.

CHAPTER 5
BE NEIGHBORLY

How did a one-time yoga instructor manage to create one of America's fastest-growing companies? Ask Michael Penny that question and he doesn't need to think long to answer.

"People can copy what we do, but they can't copy us," said Michael. "It's about transparency and a connection with the customer."

Michael was 51 when he started Savvy Rest, an organic mattress and bedding manufacturer based in Charlottesville, Virginia. Since the company began operations in 2006, annual revenue has risen from just under $400,000 that year to $5.6 million in 2012. Savvy Rest, whose distribution network now has more than 100 dealers, made *Inc.* magazine's list of America's 500/5000 fastest-growing private companies four years in a row since 2009.

As the chief executive of a multi-million-dollar company, Michael is in a far different place now than he was earlier in his life. For almost 20 years, he taught yoga in the ashram where he lived with his family. When they left in 1994, Michael's transition from a quiet, secluded religious community into the outside world – where he had to find a new way to make a living – wasn't easy.

Eventually, Michael found a job with a futon company, where he says he learned "a lot of secrets about the mattress industry," including its selling techniques.

"I had some sense of how people wanted to be treated," he said. "They're tired of tricks."

When he started his own mattress business, Michael used this insight to adopt a different customer service approach that he calls "Savvy Selling." He describes it as "a way of selling authentically, treating your customer like a neighbor or a friend, treating her or him the way you would want to be treated." When training new Savvy Rest salespeople, he emphasizes the importance of making each customer "feel safe, warm and welcomed."

A desire to provide the best customer service possible is a trait shared by many successful late-blooming entrepreneurs. In some cases, this passion originates from years spent in corporations that provided regular customer service training. Depending upon what they learned, the entrepreneurs from this world may adopt these customer service techniques and philosophies as their own or, like Michael Penny, use them to decide what *not* to do.

More often than not, however, the drive for great customer service comes from something that can't be taught in a training seminar. For late bloomers, the biggest influence and motivator is their life experience – and the fact they've been customers themselves for so long.

In their professional and personal lives, they've waited in lines, been put on hold indefinitely or stood at a counter while a salesperson on a personal phone call ignored them. They've also encountered employees who greeted them with a warm smile, went out of their way to accommodate a special request or responded promptly when something went wrong. In short, they've seen the good, the bad and the ugly of customer service and they know, from firsthand experience, what makes customers happy and unhappy.

Now, as entrepreneurs, they're channeling their life experience into their businesses by treating their own customers the way *they* want to be treated – in a friendly, *neighborly* way. Given its effect on the bottom line, it's a principle worth adopting for your own business.

As you'll read in this chapter, the application of this service philosophy isn't limited to the way employees answer the telephone or handle a returned purchase. It also surfaces in many behind-the scenes functions – from administrative procedures to relationships with vendors and employees – to ensure everything comes together to create a positive, enjoyable experience for the customer.

WHAT'S IT MEAN TO BE "NEIGHBORLY"?

For businesses, the neighbor comparison works two ways. It means not only *treating* customers the same way as a neighbor but *being* one as well.

That dual role comes easily to late bloomers, who have an inclination to embrace humanitarianism. As people age, and realize their time left in the world is limited, they may develop a desire to "make a positive difference" and give back to their communities.

Many entrepreneurs interviewed for this book are current or former volunteers. Prestige Limousine's Rory Kelly enjoys working with the elderly. Bill Cheeks of ABBA Associates stays active in several youth organizations. Card Alert Services' Richard Urban is a one-time hospice worker and a supporter of rebuilding efforts in third-world countries. Julie Savitt of AMS Earth Movers is a mentor for young entrepreneurs.

Among the most active volunteers is TechGuard

Security's Suzanne Magee. Her long list of affiliations includes serving as a board member for the State of Missouri's Small Business Development Center. She's also participated in the FBI's InfraGuard and the cybersecurity review efforts initiated by the Clinton and Obama administrations. "For me, volunteer work is personally rewarding," Suzanne said. "It's in giving that you receive."

One of the most recognized examples of a company embracing neighborly service is State Farm, whose slogan – "Like a good neighbor, State Farm is there" – is also the insurance company's catchy jingle (written by pop music legend Barry Manilow in 1971).[1] Another big corporate name associated with neighborly service is Disney, which has a program – Disney Good Neighbor Hotels – for hotels that are located near its theme parks and meet certain quality and service standards set by the company.[2]

In addition to Disney and State Farm, thousands of restaurants, pharmacies, housing facilities, legal practices, utility companies and other entities include "good neighbor" in their company names, products or services. Why do so many businesses want to come across as neighborly?

It's an interesting question, especially since the word "neighbor" doesn't always have a positive connotation. If you live in an apartment building or condominium, for example, your idea of a "good neighbor" might be one you never see or hear. You might not know your neighbors if you live in an area with a high percentage of dual-income households. After all, block parties and other gatherings become more difficult to plan (and attend) when everybody works long hours.

Thankfully, the old-fashioned notion of a good neighbor isn't totally obsolete. Businesses seem to align themselves with the images portrayed in popular 1950s, '60s and '70s TV shows like "Happy Days," "Leave It to Beaver" and "Mayberry RFD" – whose neighborhood settings gave the flavor for most plots. The shows' characters welcomed new residents with a pie and helped friends who lived on the street whenever they got in a jam. In today's fast-paced society, close-knit communities still exist where people know and watch out for one another – and maybe get together for an occasional potluck dinner.

How can a business owner incorporate this model into customer service policies? The first step is to understand what it means for a business to be "neighborly," a somewhat subjective term. From the comments of the entrepreneurs interviewed for this book, however, neighborly customer service includes these basic elements:

DEPENDABILITY

When it comes to the qualities of an ideal neighbor, dependability is near or at the top of the list. A car won't start, or a heavy tree limb falls on a fence. A key ingredient for a cake recipe isn't in the pantry. In those types of situations, most people (even those who like their privacy) appreciate neighbors they can depend on for a jumpstart, a chainsaw, a cup of sugar or other help.

Dependability is a prized quality in companies as well. The best companies, and most successful entrepreneurs, know that dependability means *consistency* in the service experience. Whether your customer buys something next week, next month or next year, you want him or her to receive excellent service and quality – each and every time.

But even with quality products, something can go awry. If a new dishwasher breaks or a component for a just-delivered heater is missing, no customer wants to be left hanging. The company that comes through and acts quickly to fix problems is the one that wins its customer's appreciation. Add a sincere apology and a 20 percent off coupon to the mix – and the company is sure to get the customer's business the next time.

For late-blooming entrepreneurs, consistent service and problem-solving matter as well. In addition, dependability means delivering services or products on time and within budget. It means not just meeting expectations but *exceeding* them. "I love to know that we did a great job," said AMS Earth Movers' Julie Savitt. "I love getting letters from clients. The greatest reward is that we know what we did was successful."

HOSPITALITY

"One of the things we do is that we treat people as if they were coming into our home," said Franny Martin of Cookies on Call. So does Prestige Limousine's Rory Kelly. The seating areas of his limos include cold bottled water, magazines and other thoughtful touches for the comfort and enjoyment of his passengers.

Other late bloomers follow variations of this theme. They greet customers with a smile, take their coats and offer them coffee – just as they do for a neighbor who stops by their house. They may provide waiting areas with TVs, restrooms with diaper-changing tables or other accommodations with customer hospitality in mind. Ideally, these offerings make customers feel appreciated. They leave happy and look forward to their next visit.

PERSONAL ATTENTION

Any company seeking to provide a service experience that's "neighborly" *has* to provide personal attention to its customers. Use of names, eye contact and polite inquiries about family or job all are ways to do this. Knowledge about repeat customers' likes and dislikes also is key. Who doesn't love it (or feel flattered) when a salesperson recalls the details of a past purchase, or a preference for a certain brand or color?

For Savvy Rest's Michael Penny, personal attention means listening to his customers and "feeling" their needs. "I don't try to sell them on any particular product," said Michael. "I let them tell me what they need and whether they have certain physical conditions [pregnancy, joint problems, injuries, etc.] that need addressing."

In customer service, the opposite of personal attention is the feeling that you're just another number – something that the best late-blooming entrepreneurs take steps to avoid. Great Harvest Bread Company's Bonnie Alton doesn't have an office in her bakery because she's observed too many people who use their office to escape. "When I am at the bakery," said Bonnie, "I can physically do the work and focus on what matters most – the customers and the staff."

WARMTH

From 1968 until 2001, Mr. Rogers' Neighborhood, hosted by Fred Rogers, was a beloved public television show for millions of children.[3] Each show began with Rogers singing "Won't You Be My Neighbor?" as he entered his house and exchanged a business jacket and dress shoes for a sweater and sneakers. Rogers invited his young viewers into his living room and, with his appearance, tone of voice and friendly manner, made them feel welcome and comfortable.

Kids made up the target audience for Mr. Rogers' Neighborhood but the kindness and caring warmth exuded by Rogers appeal to people of all ages. Smart business people can learn something about interpersonal communications by watching reruns of the show.

In general, people who start businesses later in life truly care about the wellbeing of their customers – just as they care about their friends, family and neighbors. It shows in the way these business owners interact with customers and the one-on-one connection they establish with many of them.

Patemm founder Grace Welch's comments about customer service are typical of these entrepreneurs. "I love talking to my customers," she said. "Your customers are your best salespeople. I've always reached out to them."

Sometimes, entrepreneurs realize they aren't the company's best customer representative, so they delegate that role. "Having been a customer all my life, I am passionate about customer service but I'm not good at it," said Barbara Cosgrove, the founder of Barbara Cosgrove Lamps. "That job was taken away from me. I always hire people who are better than I am."

WHAT ABOUT ONLINE BUSINESSES?

A brick-and-mortar business has many ways to implement a neighborly feel. The right lighting, color schemes, wall hangings and other decorative touches can create a home-like ambiance. So can a comfortable lounging area, a place to hang a coat and an offer for a cup of coffee or tea.

None of those things is possible for an online operation, a fact that smart brick-and-mortar businesses use as a competitive advantage. They can't always beat the prices offered by some virtual competitors but their employees can still shake hands with the people who come in the front door.

Given the absence of physical contact with customers, can an online business offer neighborly customer service? The answer is yes, but the business needs to pay attention to the tone of its visual, written, verbal and electronic communications. "You can give eye contact by the inflection in your voice," said Bill West, principal of Dallas, Texas-based WMC Marketing Partners, whose expertise includes relationship marketing programs for financial services companies.

You can also create vivid imagery with the right words, as any good copywriter knows. When Grace Welch launched Patemm, her online diaper pad company, she used email to disseminate a decisively neighborly message: "the birth of my newest baby."

Another option for both online and brick-and-mortar businesses is to foster a sense of community through an interactive Facebook Fan page where the business and its customers can post comments, images and other information.

While e-commerce offers many positives for consumers, one downside is the feeling of dealing with a faceless, impersonal entity. Often, emails sent to a company via its website go to a customer service department, rather than an individual, and receive an automated response (if any).

Sometimes an online business tries to come across as more human by creating a virtual personality – maybe a smiling person with a headset appearing under a headline such as: "Have a question? Ask Amy, our online customer service representative." Other companies, however, make it easy for customers to reach a real, live person whenever they want to.

Among the companies who subscribe to this policy is L.L. Bean, whose multi-channel retail operation includes a big Internet presence. In a September 2010 interview with the National Retail Federation, President and CEO Chris McCormick discussed his company's commitment to satisfying its customers and described what it does differently from other companies. "We believe in personal, prompt service, which is why we answer the majority of our calls within 20 seconds and always with a live person," said McCormick. The company responds to emails and chats, he added, and sees social media as "yet another opportunity to engage customers and build brand awareness."[4]

Successful late-blooming entrepreneurs also believe in the importance of live contact with customers, even when they're Internet-based or do a large percentage of business online. "People think an online presence is the easiest thing to do, but it isn't," said Graystone Industries' John Olson. "You have to spend time with your customers."

It isn't difficult to reach Patemm's Grace Welch on

the phone – something that surprises and delights her customers. Barbara Cosgrove Lamps handles its consumer business online but a receptionist answers the phone at its headquarters. Cookies on Call owner Franny Martin has a website with her complete contact information and this message for her customers: "Keeping you happy is very important to me. Always know you may contact me with any comments you may have…. I promise you will receive a response directly from me… ALWAYS!"

WHY GREAT CUSTOMER SERVICE DEPENDS UPON SUPPLIERS

When it comes to customer service, people usually focus on areas that involve direct contact with the customer. That's understandable, since the way employees greet people, answer questions, respond to requests or handle concerns can determine whether a customer returns.

But to succeed in providing a great customer experience, entrepreneurs have to think holistically. That means paying close attention to mundane aspects of their business that the public never sees (and doesn't care about).

One of those aspects is the wholesale, supply and delivery operations of a business, an area where owners may base decisions on price alone. If supplier B offers to sell a key component at five cents per unit less than supplier A, that's enough for some companies to make a switch. It's a short-sighted way to look at vendor relationships, which have everything to do with meeting customers' expectations and providing a service experience that's memorable for the right reasons. The reason is simple: Without vendors, you've got nothing to sell (usually).

In some business circles, companies subscribe to the saying, "you're only as good as your worst supplier." The best entrepreneurs understand this, which is why they don't see their vendors and suppliers as just deliverers of parts or support services. They see them as valued business partners who are critical for their own companies' success.

Likewise, the best vendors strive to take care of their commercial customers and offer programs that help them become more profitable, a message conveyed by Trek Bicycle president John Burke in a February 2012 email to the company's dealers. "One piece of advice I would give to retailers is to go through your supply chain and see who your suppliers are and who your partners are," said Burke. "I would do as much business as possible with your partners."

Graystone Industries' John Olson is another business owner who sees himself as not just a supplier but a partner. In 2009, Graystone moved its headquarters from Florida to Georgia after John purchased an executive retreat in foreclosure. The site underwent a multi-million-dollar renovation in 2010 that added a new retail store/showroom and other ancillary structures. A 3,700-square-foot warehouse to service the Atlanta market began operations in 2012 (the company has another 7,400-square-foot warehouse in Franklin, North Carolina, that serves other areas in the Southeast region).

The Graystone complex – which has conference space and guest rooms, along with its other amenities – reflects one of John Olson's primary goals: to help others prosper and enjoy the type of lifestyle he has. He plans to host meetings so industry colleagues and their families can convene to learn and relax, which he sees as a win-win. "The more I can help my business customers grow, the more they are going to buy from me," he said.

EMPLOYEES DESERVE
NEIGHBORLY SERVICE, TOO

Vendor and supplier relationships aren't the only ones that affect a company's ability to deliver on customer service. What matters – a lot – are a business owner's relationships with employees. If you want your customers to receive service that is hospitable, reliable, personal and warm, treat your staff the same way.

A believer in this thinking is Sharon Dillard, the president of a family-owned business you'll read about later. While she uses "family" rather than "neighbor" to characterize how she views her employees, the basic idea is the same.

"We treat all employees like family, not just the four who are," she said. "Our open door policy allows any employee access to decision makers to bounce off ideas or just to say good morning. This is also how we treat customers and suppliers."

For some, that idea may seem strange. A business owner could say: Why would I treat the people I hire like family or neighbors? I pay them a salary and give them benefits. In a tough economy where it's hard to find a job, that ought to be enough.

Maybe that attitude is okay if you don't mind when your staff leaves for better opportunities. But it isn't if you want to attract and retain quality employees who can help you build an exceptional organization.

Consider The Ritz-Carlton Hotel Company and its motto: "We are ladies and gentlemen serving ladies and gentlemen."[5] Isn't that a good indicator of how a company world-renowned for its customer service views its employees?

This is an area where the Golden Rule matters big-time. How management interacts with employees has *everything* to do with how they, in turn, interact with customers. No one understands this better than late-blooming entrepreneurs do. Just as they've been customers for a long time, they've also been employees – often with bad bosses, limited growth opportunities or other unsatisfying situations that contributed to their decision to go out on their own.

"When I was working in a full-time job, it was a bit discouraging when people didn't get promoted when they deserved to be," said Drawing Conclusions' Donna Herrle.

Still, even well-treated employees don't always work out. When that happens, late bloomers tend to cut their losses quickly, knowing it's less painful than hoping the situation will turn itself around. They take care of – and give credit to – good employees, knowing their loyalty, dedication and motivation will pay dividends in many ways.

Listen to the late bloomers talk about their employees and you can tell how much they care about them. "Part of my success is finally finding the right people, people who share my passion and know about marketing," said Franny Martin of Cookies on Call. "They actually think about it as a business, not just a place where they work."

THE BOTTOM LINE: STICK WITH THE BASICS

By the time they reach 40, most people have been through at least one difficult time in their lives, such as a divorce, a serious illness, or the death of a family member or close friend. When you've endured hardships, little annoyances don't get to you as much. That makes it easier to put customer service situations into perspective and resolve issues in a patient, friendly manner.

"As they age, most people mellow to some extent and are more likely to be able to handle some of the less intelligent questions often asked of customer service representatives," said Art Koff of RetiredBrains.com.

Forty-and-older entrepreneurs also have plenty of experience navigating sometimes-tricky relationships with coworkers, supervisors, direct reports and customers – all of which helps on the customer service side. "I could not have run a company as a younger man. I did not have the experience or wisdom," said Graystone Industries' John Olson.

"It took years of working to cultivate the kind of customer service expertise I have now."

Not every late-blooming entrepreneur considers himself or herself to be good at customer service. When they aren't, they may manage this weakness in the same way as lamp entrepreneur Barbara Cosgrove – by finding partners or employees who are better at it than they are. Regardless of whether they possess these skills personally, they're passionate about offering the best service possible for those who support their businesses.

"You have to honor your customers," said Franny Martin. John Olson concurs. "Everything that I do has value to the customer," he said.

Neighborly service isn't complicated but it does take devotion, a quality that late bloomers bring to the table. Unlike their younger counterparts, who often start businesses with the intent to sell them, they're usually in it for the long haul. During the interviews for this book, one or two entrepreneurs mentioned selling their companies at some point, but their reasons had to do with retiring (finally) rather than making money. They have an emotional investment in what they're doing – which manifests itself in the way they treat their customers.

In the end, providing your customer with service that's neighborly means exactly that – extending hospitality, reliability, personal attention and warmth to make customers feel a certain way. Unfortunately, it's an approach that seems to be missing from many companies, including some that invest big money in sophisticated operating systems, training programs and high-tech gadgetry intended to make them more profitable.

"The trouble with businesses today is that they think they've invented everything," said Bill West, the Dallas-based marketing consultant. "The basics are the basics. Treat people just the way you want to be treated."

Remember that as you go forward. *Be neighborly.* If you do, your customers, suppliers and employees will love you. You'll be rewarded with repeat business and positive word-of-mouth advertising – and will be well on your way to joining the ranks of successful entrepreneurs.

NOW WHAT? 10 WAYS TO TAKE ACTION

1. Make your customers feel welcome when they visit your business. Greet each person who comes through the door. Offer light refreshments and a comfortable place to sit, along with other touches of hospitality.

2. Be a good neighbor yourself. Volunteer for local causes. Support your community. It's the right thing to do – and it will be good for your business.

3. Be accessible. When customers contact your business, make it easy for them to reach a real, live person if they want to.

4. Get to know your customers. Ask about their jobs and families. Keep an up-to-date record of their brand, color and/or style preferences in your computer system. Personalized service generates sales.

5. Use people's names as much as possible. This includes emails to customers. A message addressed to "Dear Valued Customer" doesn't exactly convey a personal feeling.

6. Make sure everyone in management stays in touch with the customer. Have managers answer the phone, work on the sales floor or do other jobs that get them away from their computers and interacting with customers.

7. Respond quickly if something goes wrong with a product or service. If you are at fault, apologize. Dependable companies that take responsibility and fix problems promptly

are the ones that will win customers' appreciation – and repeat business.

8. Find out what your customers think about your service. Ask them directly through surveys. Monitor social media sites regularly to see what they're saying. Remember: It's what your customers think, not what you think, that matters.

9. View everyone in your organization as being in customer service, from the office manager who does the books to the employee sweeping the floors. In one way or another, each staff member affects the customer's experience.

10. Remember that customers aren't the only ones who deserve neighborly service. Treat your vendors and employees the same way. Remember the Golden Rule. Be neighborly!

CHAPTER 6
STAY ON THE TIGER

Has a life-changing event inspired you to start your own business? If so, you're in good company.

Franny Martin decided to start her online cookie company after a visit with her seriously ill father. Donna Herrle launched Drawing Conclusions as a full-time graphic design company after a job layoff. David Drewry began his home inspection business after a military promotion didn't happen.

Maybe an epiphany of similar magnitude has given you a kick in the pants. You recognize that life is short, so you've decided to stop dreaming about becoming an entrepreneur – and do something about it. If that's the case, feel good about taking that first step.

Right now, motivation isn't a problem. If you're like most people about to start a business, you're pumped about the opportunities and lifestyle changes it will bring. But once the novelty wears off – and reality sets in – it becomes tough to *stay* pumped day in and day out. Maybe that's why many entrepreneurs featured in these pages say tenacity is critical to succeed as a business owner.

Back in Chapter 3, Barbara Cosgrove, founder of Barbara Cosgrove Lamps, described the need for tenacity this way: "Someone said to me, 'this business is like a tiger. If you get off, it will eat you.' You have to figure out how to stay on."

Compared with other traits that a successful business owner needs, how important is an ability to "stay on the tiger" and keep going no matter what? Studies suggest it's the one personal quality shared by leaders in every field. In 2007, a team of academic researchers published a report that examined the connection between high achievement and "grit," which they defined as "perseverance and passion for long-term goals."[1] Grit, they concluded, outweighs intelligence as a predictor of success.

Isn't that the truth! Ever known people who did well in school, then fizzled once they got into the real world? Maybe they were lacking in the grit department.

If you belong to a gym, you've seen what happens in January. For the first two weeks, the place is packed with people who have vowed to exercise and/or lose weight as a New Year's Resolution. By Week 3, most of these folks aren't coming any longer. They decide running on a treadmill or lifting weights every week is boring or too much work, so they give up and revert to eating potato chips on the couch while watching TV.

The same thing happens in entrepreneurship. Some of the very first steps, like naming the business or coming up with a slogan, are fun and exciting. *Then* comes a long list of operational tasks. Among them: finding startup money; applying for permits; establishing inventory and payroll systems; and hiring and managing employees. You also have to become familiar with certain laws and regulations and deal with a stack of administrative and legal paperwork that definitely isn't "fun." No wonder so many would-be business owners abandon ship at this point.

In the 2007 report on grit, the researchers defined "achievement" as "the product of talent and effort, the latter a function of intensity, direction and duration of one's exertions toward a goal."[2] The operative word here is "duration." Successful business ownership is an achievement that requires a sustained, focused effort over time.

That last sentence is key, so it's worth repeating.

Successful business ownership is an achievement that requires a sustained, focused effort over time.

"A lot of people have ideas but they don't implement them," said Annie Margulis of Girls Golf. "You have to stick with it. A brand doesn't happen overnight."

She's right. When it comes to meeting challenges, the world has more talkers than doers. If you're like Franny Martin, Donna Herrle or David Drewry, something's happened to light a fire within you. How can you take it to the next level – and join the select group that *follows through* and turns an idea into a real and successful business? How can you become a doer, rather than just another talker?

That's what this chapter is about. In it, you'll read about tenacity, including why it's so difficult to maintain, when it's most needed and what established entrepreneurs do to keep themselves going. But the most important message can be found in Annie Margulis' words. A brand – or a business – doesn't happen overnight. More often than not, products or companies that seem to surface suddenly have been in the works for a while. The process to bring a business idea to market can take a *lot* longer than you think, so be prepared for that reality.

THE BIGGEST TENACITY BUSTERS

Three out of 10 "employer firms" (businesses with paid employment and a payroll) don't survive for two years, says the U.S. Small Business Administration. Only half survive at least five years. Why do so many throw in the towel early in the game?

Ask five people that question and you'll get five different answers, but often it comes down to tenacity. It may evaporate because:

- Typically, you have to do almost everything yourself at the beginning. This can be both exhausting and a big adjustment, especially for those who come from corporate backgrounds and are used to having administrative help.

- You encounter complications, delays and setbacks, which can be especially frustrating if the new business involves a time-sensitive idea (i.e., you're anxious to introduce a new product or service before someone beats you to it).

- You make many mistakes. Some may be expensive, which isn't all bad if you learn from them.

- You encounter rejection at all levels – from suppliers and banks who aren't interested in dealing with a nascent company to "friends" who don't believe in you or your idea.

In addition, aspiring entrepreneurs may not last because they're unwilling to commit to the marathon effort that's normally required before any real money comes in. Tim Webb, the attorney-turned-commercial real estate marketer you met in Chapter 2, is among those who have seen this happen.

"I know a lot of people who didn't make it," said Tim. "They underestimated the difficulties and the time it would take to go from a negative to a positive cash-flow situation."

Sometimes the reasons for insufficient tenacity don't surface until the business in underway. Even when the personal desire and financial wherewithal are there, people may not stick with a business startup because:

- They lack ongoing support from their family. Spouses or life partners may be gung ho at first. But if success is slow to materialize, their enthusiasm may wane and doubts start to emerge. It's difficult to remain tenacious about a startup, or *any* major goal for that matter, when your spouse or other people you love don't have your back.

- They're procrastinators or poor time managers, or have other destructive, firmly entrenched work habits that impede their ability to stay on track.

- They're fuzzy thinkers. Without a clear vision, they spin their wheels, causing the entrepreneurial endeavor to run out of gas.

- They're overwhelmed. With so much to do, they don't know where to start or fail to start small – and consequently never get off the ground.

- They aren't truly committed and, as a result, don't dedicate the enormous time and energy required to carry things through from beginning to end.

- They have other time-consuming responsibilities and don't make business ownership a high enough priority. This is a big one for the over-40 crowd. When you're 25 and single, you can eat, sleep and breathe your startup if you want. But when you're 45 and have a family, it's all too easy to become sidetracked and lose focus.

WHEN TENACITY MATTERS THE MOST

If anything on the above list sounds overly familiar, watch out. The more you can do in advance
to resolve or weed out these tenacity busters, the
better positioned you'll be for the months and
years ahead.

The business owners featured in this book relied
upon their tenacity to get through all kinds of situations. Some owners, like Prestige Limousine's
Rory Kelly, endured unsatisfactory jobs while
transitioning into entrepreneurship. Rory, as you'll
recall, kept working in the steel industry for a couple of years as he laid the groundwork for his
limo service.

Bonnie Alton, the owner of the Great Harvest
Bread Company franchise in St. Paul, also went
through a transitioning phase recounted earlier. Each morning, she got up before dawn and
worked at the bakery for a few hours before going
on to her day job with a law firm.

Tenacity also helped these business owners
weather difficult times after they were up and
running. Bonnie Alton went through a challenging
period in 2004, when rising rent prices prompted
her to relocate her bakery. Around the same time,
the Atkins diet was in full swing, causing many

dieters to shun bread and other baked goods. "I had to do a lot of morale building," said Bonnie. "It took a couple of years to get through it all."

Likewise, tenacity – and life experience – helped home inspector David Drewry during weak stretches in the housing market. "Younger people get more concerned about dips in business because they haven't survived the peaks and valleys," he said.

You could go on for a long time looking at the myriad of situations that make tenacity so essential for starting and maintaining a business. For entrepreneurs offering unique goods or services, the most crucial time, arguably, is the product development stage.

Several people interviewed for this book mentioned the "10,000-hour rule," an idea popularized by author Malcolm Gladwell in his bestseller *"Outliers: The Story of Success."* Basically, this rule says that "the magic number for true expertise" is 10,000 hours of practice.[3] Likewise, when you're developing a cookie recipe or a diaper changing pad (as Franny Martin and Grace Welch did), you have to test, revise, test, revise and test again – until you finally get it right.

Some of the most revolutionary or popular products have come from 40-and-older inventors.

In 2011, I researched some of these inventors and wrote about them in a blog post. Martin Cooper was in his 40s when he invented the cell phone. So was Ruth Handler, one of the founders of Mattel, Inc., when she invented the Barbie doll. Henry Ford and Colonel Sanders introduced Ford cars and Kentucky Fried Chicken to the public when they were in their 40s and 60s respectively.[4] Often, these inventors went through years of failed attempts before finally succeeding.

What if they had decided: "I'm too old to do this" – then quit? Fortunately, that didn't happen. They didn't let their age, or anything else, get in the way of accomplishing their goal.

Neither did Richard Urban, a now-retired entrepreneur who cofounded a company called Card Alert Services. Richard understands just how much tenacity it takes to bring an idea to life. His entrepreneurial epiphany happened in 1992, with the discovery of a bogus ATM machine.

Back then, Richard was working for an electronic payments company whose biggest project was Money Access Service (MAC), a regional ATM network that consisted of several banks in three Pennsylvania counties. His skills and knowledge expanded significantly after he attended a two-year banking program at the University of Virginia and did his thesis on electronic banking – an area that was just beginning to get hot.

By the time 1992 arrived, Richard was in charge of new-product development, an area that included smart cards and e-banking. That January, he was flying home from a Colorado ski vacation when he struck up a conversation with a man seated next to him. His new acquaintance mentioned that he and his wife taught a four-day course on life planning. Richard and his wife signed up for the course. On the final day, each person presented his or her life plan to the other class participants.

"One of my goals was to start a business," said Richard. "I had no idea as to what type of business, but that planted a seed."

A few months later, two thieves managed to defraud hundreds of bank customers by installing a fake ATM machine in a Connecticut shopping mall. The incident revealed the banking system's vulnerability, as well as an increasing sophistication among criminals to perpetuate electronic fraud.

Richard's company asked him to lead a task force to study possible solutions to counter e-fraud. After a six-month investigation, the task force published a report and presented its findings to bank industry leaders. The estimated cost to protect the industry: a whopping $600 to $800 million.

"The industry let us know that an investment of that magnitude was not in the cards, so to speak," said Richard. "The proposal was dead on arrival."

Richard and the task force went back to the drawing board and started brainstorming based upon new criteria from the bankers. The solution, they said, had to be low-cost, easy to implement, effective – and not require changes to the existing card infrastructure.

"After several false starts, we hit upon the analogy of a fire department," says Richard. Just as the department uses sensors, rather than fireproofing, to protect city buildings from the threat of fire, financial institutions needed an early detection system to protect themselves from debit-card fraud. That "paradigm shift," as Richard describes it, eventually would lead to the formation of his own company.

Convinced that early detection was the right approach, Richard presented his idea to upper management, who said it wouldn't work. Undaunted, he pressed on until his idea "began to get legs," as he put it. He talked to others, including Doug Anderson, his long-time business associate and friend.

In 1993, Richard Urban and Doug Anderson left the company. One year later, when Richard was 51, he and Doug founded Arlington, Virginia-based Card Alert Services, which used computer software to detect unusual activity at individual ATMs.

During its first year, the nascent company had to undertake a three-month, 35-bank study that showed the existence of a fraud problem before board members of regional bank networks agreed to invest money. As this effort was underway, so were the processes to hire a software developer, obtain a patent and obtain buy-in from major financial institutions and card networks.

Eventually, these efforts paid off. By the time HNC Software acquired it in 2000, Card Alert Services had around $2.5 to $3 million dollars in gross revenue, 10,000 banks and eight networks as customers, and 45 employees.

MAINTAINING YOUR MOMENTUM: THE KEY COMPONENTS

Much of Card Alert Services' success stemmed from a well-timed product that filled an immediate need. But the company wouldn't have realized its goals – nor would Richard Urban and his business partners be where they are today – without the sticking power to get through to the end.

Still, even the Richard Urbans of the world have good days and bad days. How do the best entrepreneurs keep going when they don't feel like it? To borrow Barbara Cosgrove's comparison, how do they stay on the tiger on those days when they're ready to jump off?

Passion

Passion gives you the drive and adrenaline to keep going during difficult stretches. "The passion has to be there. You have to absolutely love it," said Cookies on Call's Franny Martin.

As pointed out in Chapter 1, passion can be a major weakness without the discipline to channel it in the right direction. When the discipline is there, however, passion can lead to desired results.

One entrepreneur who is both passionate *and* disciplined about her business is Jennifer Campbell, a personal historian and the founder of Heritage Memoirs, based in Uxbridge, Ontario. Using recorded interviews, she produces personal memoirs and family histories. Often, the final product is a bound book, providing a treasured heirloom for Jennifer's clients to pass on to family members and others close to them.

Jennifer's current compensation far exceeds what she earned before she became a business owner. More important, she loves what she's doing – and no longer has to endure a daily round-trip commute that, on some days, took several hours.

Still, her life has had its share of difficulties. In February 2008, a layoff ended her public television job of seven years. "Funding had been cut and I could see the writing on the wall," said Jennifer, "but still, it was a shock when I was let go."

On the same day as the layoff, she attended the funeral of a friend killed by a drunk driver. After the one-two punch, she knew she didn't want to spend the rest of her professional life toiling in a little gray cubicle.

"I've always had an entrepreneurial bent but the time wasn't right earlier," she said. "I was raising two boys who were going into university. Security was important to me and I wasn't ready to give that up."

A few years earlier, Jennifer began compiling personal histories for people after realizing she knew little about her own father, a Scottish immigrant and one-time soldier, when he died at age 80. Not wanting to lose both of her parents' histories,

Jennifer managed to get a few life stories from her mother, an accomplished artist, before she developed dementia and passed away.

At age 54, Jennifer turned her hobby into a business, launching Heritage Memoirs with little more than a beat-up tape recorder and a "really cheap" website. "I wasn't thinking about making a lot of money," she said. "All I wanted was something that was important work."

Recognizing she needed help with her startup, Jennifer bartered her editing skills for consulting services from a marketing coach she found through the Association of Personal Historians (APH). She also prepared a written business plan, something she recommends for aspiring business owners. Her husband, an accountant, helped with her bookkeeping setup and provided other support.

"There were really lean times at the beginning," she said. "When you're in it for the long haul, you understand peaks and valleys."

While Jennifer points to strong market demand as a top reason for her success, it also came from her commitment "to provide the best work I possibly can and go the extra mile." She sees her age as a plus, as it gives her empathy and an understanding that success doesn't happen overnight.

"If I had started the business when I was 30," said Jennifer, "I might have given up after a year."

FOCUS

While passion is the emotion needed for tenacity, it also requires a clear destination or focus. As pointed out in the "tenacity busters" list, fuzzy thinkers tend to burn out or become frustrated because they don't know where they're headed. It's like trying to run a race without knowing the location of the finish line.

Judging from the experiences of late bloomers in the business world, aspiring entrepreneurs can clarify and/or improve their goals through a combination of tactics. Among them:

- *Put goals in writing* This creates a "commitment device," which *"Freakonomics"* authors Stephen J. Dubner and Steven D. Levitt define as "a means with which to lock yourself into a course of action that you might not otherwise choose but that produces a desired result."[5] That's the power of putting your goals on paper. "If you do this, something in the brain cements it," said Jennifer Campbell.

- *Create a business plan.* When it's finished, you'll have a roadmap to achieve your goals and, hopefully, a clearly defined business idea that's different from or better than what's already out there. Rory Kelly's plan, for example, called for marketing Prestige Limousine as a backup service to a core group of other local limo companies – a targeted approach that's worked well for him. "I found a niche in the industry that allowed me to reduce advertising and marketing costs while increasing revenues and profits," said Rory.

- *Don't spread yourself too thin.* Four years after the opening of her first Great Harvest bakery, Bonnie Alton opened a second location – a "warm spot" where most of the items were made at the other bakery. After two years, she sold it. "It was an unsatisfactory experience," she said, "because it didn't allow me to spend enough time with my customers and staff at the other location."

- *Surround yourself with supportive people.* TechGuard Security's Suzanne Magee and Card Alert's Richard Urban were among those who were told their business ideas wouldn't work. Rather than being thwarted by the naysayers, they surrounded themselves with people who helped them stay on track.

- *Keep your family in the loop.* For entrepreneurs with spouses/partners or children, focus becomes extremely difficult if a key member of the household isn't on board with the startup. Regular communication goes a long way towards maintaining the family buy-in that's essential for your personal happiness and the business's growth.

- *Delegate.* "If there's any way to outsource, do so," recommended John Olson of Graystone Industries. Consultants and/or contractors may be able to handle certain day-to-day tasks, so you can focus on the big picture. Just be careful about who you hire and what you delegate. Otherwise, outsourcing might become more trouble than it's worth.

TIME MANAGEMENT

The people in this book lead lives filled with dead-lines, appointments, phone calls and emails. They have bills to pay, houses to maintain and personal obligations to meet – just like the rest of us. How can they do all those things and still run their businesses effectively?

Time management helps – a lot. Remember Tim Webb's comments back in Chapter 2? He's a big proponent of the 80-20 principle – i.e., spend 80 percent of your time on the 20 percent that matters the most. That step alone will go a *long* way to help any entrepreneur achieve key goals.

In addition, many business owners are members of the unofficial early risers club. They get up at five o'clock in the morning (or earlier) to take advantage of the fewer interruptions and distractions that occur before the workday's traditional 9 a.m. start. RetiredBrains's Art Koff, for example, usually starts answering emails around 6:30 a.m.

Good time managers also learn to say no to things that don't move the ball. An item that falls into this category sometimes is social media. Sure, it can help you connect with long-lost contacts and generate new business. But when it becomes addictive or a favorite way to procrastinate (who wouldn't rather catch up with friends on Facebook than review financial statements?), it turns into a major time waster.

One entrepreneur who had time-management

challenges at the beginning is Drawing Conclusions' Donna Herrle. "I found that I was so anxious to get clients that I was spending all my time in meetings," she said. "Someone advised me to protect one day a week where there are no meetings." Now, that's what she does.

EXERCISE

"Being physically fit gives you discipline," said St. Paul Great Harvest Bread Company's Bonnie Alton, an avid runner and cyclist. "It takes a certain amount of tenacity to keep running when you're hurting. I believe those traits carry over to starting a business."

Not all late-blooming entrepreneurs exercise regularly, but many do. Like Bonnie, they believe physical fitness increases their stamina and provides other health benefits that improve the overall quality of their lives. They also like the challenge and satisfaction that come from setting and meeting personal fitness goals. Donna Herrle, for example, aims to complete a century (100-mile) bicycle ride each year.

Several late bloomers also mentioned mental health as a key reason why they exercise. "I walk almost every day, usually a couple of miles in the evening," said ABBA Associates' Bill Cheeks, who also follows a vitamin regimen and drinks a lot of water. "It gets me out and clears my head."

"QUITTERS NEVER WIN AND WINNERS NEVER QUIT"

If this chapter did its job, it led to more introspection. Are you passionate about your business idea? Do you know where you want to go? Do you have supportive friends and family who will help you stay on track? Can you manage your time to focus on what matters – and say "no" to what doesn't? Do you need to exercise more and/or eat better to boost your stamina?

Most important, do you have the tenacity and grit to weather the frustration, rejection and failure that are inevitable in entrepreneurship?

Don't sell yourself short on the last question. The older you are, the grittier you tend to be, found the 2007 report on grit and achievement. The researchers' intuition was that "one learns from experience that quitting plans, shifting goals, and starting over repeatedly are not good strategies for success." [6]

But sometimes you *do* have to start over to succeed in the end. Maybe you've heard the story about a young reporter who interviewed Thomas Edison shortly before he discovered a successful filament for the light bulb. While variations exist, the basic story goes like this: The reporter asked Edison whether it was time to give up, since he had failed thousands of times. Edison replied that he hadn't failed. He had just found thousands of ways that an electric light bulb wouldn't work!

For a contemporary example of tenacity, think about Apple's Steve Jobs. His brilliant career produced the iPod, iPad, iTunes and much more. But it also included products like Lisa, a computer that cost tens of millions of dollars to develop and ended up going nowhere.[7]

You may have an idea for a business with huge potential. But it will have no chance of succeeding unless you deal with setbacks and *stay on the tiger*. The entrepreneurs in this book are proof of this principle.

Remember the magazine item that young Franny Martin received from her father? "Quitters never win and winners never quit," the clipping read. You have to be willing to do everything you can to obtain success.

Are you?

NOW WHAT? 10 WAYS TO TAKE ACTION

1. Change how you look at failures. See them as learning experiences to figure out what didn't work.

2. Evaluate why you were, or weren't, able to reach other long-term goals in your life. Your answers could be predictors of whether you'll succeed as an entrepreneur.

3. Create a "commitment device" by writing down your main goals and putting them in a place where you'll see them every day.

4. Maintain a fitness level that will give you the stamina to handle the physical and mental demands of entrepreneurship. Find a form of exercise you like, so you'll stick with it.

5. Go back and re-read business, motivational and time-management books that are on your shelf. Now that you're in a different role (i.e., an aspiring entrepreneur), you'll see things in a different light – and pick up on ideas you missed or that didn't matter the first time.

6. Build a series of victories along the way. Map your journey so you'll recognize when

you've reached measurable milestones, then reward yourself for doing so.

7. Surround yourself with people who believe in you – and who will support you no matter what.

8. Break big projects into smaller, manageable pieces.

9. Limit your use of social media. Don't let it distract you from focusing on priorities related to your startup.

10. For tenacity's sake, take a break from time to time. Go away for a long weekend or spend a day outdoors, away from any cell phones or computers. When you return to work, you'll be recharged.

CHAPTER 7
WATCH THE MONEY

Burnt out on the rat race, many of us fantasize about getting away from it all and starting a new life in a different, more relaxed place. Sharon Dillard didn't just fantasize. She made it happen.

Sharon is president of Get A Grip, a family-owned franchise company that refinishes kitchen counter-tops and bathtubs. When she isn't working, she loves riding her horse on long trail rides in the mountains. Evening walks with her dogs provide another way for her to enjoy the outdoors.

The Dillards could have built their business from anywhere in the country. They chose Albuquerque because "we love and appreciate the New Mexico lifestyle – relaxed and with an emphasis on quality of life, plus great weather," Sharon said.

It's a big change from her former life in Dallas, Texas, where Sharon spent 17 years as a cosmetics executive before starting Get A Grip in 2001. "I'd reached a point in my career where I was looking for something to challenge me and engage my curiosity," she said.

In 1998, her son Ryan took a break from college to think about the direction of his life and visit family in New Mexico. During his trip, he discovered resurfacing, a process that allows the restoration of worn bathtubs and countertops without removing them.

Recognizing the growth potential of the resurfacing business, Ryan Dillard urged his parents to come check it out for themselves. So Sharon went to New Mexico – and saw immediately what was making her son so excited. Adding to the scenario's appeal was the prospect of living in an area with such natural beauty. "Everything seemed to fall into place," she said.

Soon she began dividing her time between Dallas and Albuquerque. Six months later, she left her executive position to begin concentrating on marketing and advertising for Get A Grip. Her husband, Cub, also joined the company, bringing 30 years of sales and finance experience. Eventually, her other son, Austen, came on board as well.

Today, Get A Grip has 27 franchises and dealers in 17 states. Since 2007, when it began offering franchises, the company has been on Entrepreneur's Franchise 500 list of franchise companies in the

United States and Canada, currently ranking No. 316.

Sharon Dillard's story has a theme that's common for late-blooming entrepreneurs: Their No. 1 goal isn't to make big bucks. They want to enjoy what they're doing and get the most out of what life has to offer.

In September 2011, Encore.org (then called Civic Ventures) teamed with the MetLife Foundation to ask 1,000 Americans between the ages of 44 and 70 about their interest in starting their own business or nonprofit organization in the next five or 10 years. Among the findings: Potential "encore entrepreneurs" are driven by working on something they "are passionate about" (84 percent) and by "a sense of meaning and a feeling of accomplishment" (83 percent).[1]

Still, any entrepreneur who wants to succeed has to *watch the money*. "In the business world, money is the benchmark of success and tells you if you are doing well and how you can do better," said John Olson of Graystone Industries.

Money also tells you whether people like what you're selling. The more your customers spend on your product or service, the stronger the affirmation that it has appeal and value. High customer demand is immensely gratifying, especially for entrepreneurs who have put their blood, sweat and tears into their own inventions.

"My favorite part about owning a business is seeing someone wearing one of my outfits," said Girls Golf's Annie Margulis, who also enjoys the ability to arrange her schedule so she can play golf herself.

In addition, money matters for another, critical reason: Your business won't last if it isn't profitable. Like the majority of the Encore.org survey participants, your attraction to entrepreneurship may relate to a passion, a cause, your family or other reasons that have nothing to do with money. But you can't sustain any of these objectives unless the math works – i.e., you make more money than you spend.

Keeping a close eye on the numbers doesn't mean you can't enjoy your business – or make time for family, a charity or whatever matters to you outside work. Prestige Limousine's Rory Kelly said his definition of successful entrepreneurship is a motto he learned from his days in the steel industry. A one-time boss taught him to "be profitable and have fun doing it."

Just about all of entrepreneurs in this book share Rory's philosophy. Their experiences suggest that businesses tend to reap *greater* financial rewards when their owners care about lifestyle and treat those around them accordingly.

"Work/life balance is important to us as a company and something we emphasize with all employees," said Sharon Dillard. "It is part of the reason for our steady growth, the low turnover of our employees, and our ability to purchase a new headquarters building in the middle of a recession."

But as demonstrated by Get A Grip, another major success determinant is *the amount of discipline applied to the finance side.* "We work hard, especially in a struggling economy, to control the costs of supplies for franchises and dealers," said Sharon. "Without them, we have no business."

In this chapter, you'll read about personal finance and retirement, along with some ways that successful late-blooming entrepreneurs control expenses and manage cash flow. As their experiences show, a close watch on the money – or not – often is what separates business owners who make it from those who don't. The insights and ideas in the following pages may help you be among those who do.

OVERLOOK THIS AND YOU COULD BE IN TROUBLE

If you did the self-evaluation covered in Chapter 2, you thought about how much you know (or don't know) about accounting or bookkeeping, as well as the financial resources you have to put towards your startup. Maybe you also considered your experience with past office projects and your track record for completing them within their dollar limits.

But did you ask yourself how well you've been able to stick with a household budget (if you have one in the first place)?

What about your credit cards? Did you think about how often you've been late on your monthly bills? Or didn't pay them at all?

How's your credit report? Does it show negative information that wouldn't allow you to get a loan, or require you to pay high borrowing rates? If you don't know, better go to www.annualcreditreport.com and request a copy of your report from at least one of the three major credit bureaus (you can check your report for free once every 12 months).

If you didn't include these questions in your strengths/weaknesses analysis, you aren't alone. While it almost seems counterintuitive, personal finance acumen isn't even on the radar for some aspiring entrepreneurs.

In 2012, almost 1.2 million Americans filed for bankruptcy protection, says the Administrative Office of the U.S. Courts.[2] While the average credit-card debt per borrower has dropped in recent years, it was just under $5,000 for 2013's first quarter, reports TransUnion, one of the national credit bureaus.[3] These numbers, along with other indicators, suggest that plenty of people – including those who are 40 or older and own businesses – never master important personal finance basics.

Does the management of your own money say anything about your odds for success as an entrepreneur? Not everybody interviewed for this book thinks it does. Graystone Industries' John Olson, for example, has little interest in his personal finances and lets his wife, who oversees the business's bookkeeping, handle them. "To me, one has little to do with the other," said John, "but I suppose there are people who will strongly agree" with the idea that they do correlate.

One of them is ABBA Associates' Bill Cheeks, who stresses the importance of awareness in his personal finance seminars and applies that advice to his own business. "I always know how much money I have coming in and manage expenses very, very carefully," he said. "I spend my customers' funds as carefully as my own."

Another entrepreneur who agrees with the personal finance-entrepreneurship connection is Donna Herrle of Drawing Conclusions. "That seems consistent with all the entrepreneurs I know and have spoken to," she said.

If you ever need a business loan from a bank, your financial history *will* be a factor that determines approval, said Bill Ridenour, president of John Marshall Bank based in Reston, Virginia. "The most successful entrepreneurs have done their homework, are realistic about the risks and understand how to evaluate them," he added. "They're prepared to meet those challenges when they occur."

Among the groups that have participated in Bill Cheeks' seminars are entrepreneurs looking to expand their operations. "So many of these business owners are having credit challenges," said Bill. "They can't go to a bank to get financing because they don't pay their own bills on time. They also don't understand the importance of credit scores and good credit."

Given how much entrepreneurial self-assessment you've done already, you may be tired of it and ready to move on. But if you share Rory Kelly's vision to "be profitable and have fun doing it," you owe it to yourself to gauge your personal finance behavior. If there's ever been a time to be totally honest about your money tendencies, it's now!

Hopefully, your financial assessment will show that, after years of homeownership, budgeting and credit use, you possess money-management experience and habits that will benefit your business.

To get started, see the "Assessing Your Personal Finance Skills" sidebar at the end of this chapter.

HOW RETIREMENT FITS INTO THE PICTURE

More people in their 40s, 50s and beyond are turning to entrepreneurship for economic reasons, including ones related to retirement. Some of these new entrepreneurs lost their jobs before they accrued enough money in their IRAs or 401(k)s to fund their golden years.

Others retired voluntarily but need to bolster nest eggs eroded by inflation, meager interest rates and declining home prices (especially if they counted on the equity in their homes as a source of retirement funds). Still others want to keep working as long as possible because they're worried about outliving their savings.

Many of the business owners featured in this book became entrepreneurs for lifestyle reasons, rather than economic ones. They have zero interest in spending the second half of their lives in a rocking chair or doing activities you're "supposed" to do when you retire. "People sometimes ask me: Why are you still working?" said Bill Cheeks, the

68-year-old president of ABBA Associates. "I'm working because I'm not good at retirement."

Neither is Annie Margulis, who created the Girls Golf clothing line after she left a long nursing career. "I didn't see myself playing bridge and going out to lunch," she said.

Still, that doesn't mean Annie, Bill and the other entrepreneurs don't expect to ease up one day. Like other Americans, they want to be comfortable and not worry about money when the time arrives. They want their businesses to help them reach this goal.

That gets to a primary money question for just about every late-blooming entrepreneur: Should you use retirement money to fund your startup?

"We did not borrow from our retirement funds," said Elizabeth Erlandson of Licorice International, a candy business. "We used money from other investments, the sale of a rental property and a small inheritance."

"We were able to start very economically by running the business out of our homes," added Ardith Stuertz, Elizabeth's business partner. "Since we weren't sure how it was going to turn out, we did not go into debt and used personal resources. It was a very wise thing."

Drawing Conclusions' Donna Herrle has a view

on retirement funds that's less black and white. "Personally, I would not do it, given the fact that we are now living longer and it is difficult to determine just how much is needed for retirement," said Donna. "However, if someone has accounts that are overfunded or exceptionally healthy, it could be a viable option, assuming their business plan and concept are solid and would not require consistent draw on the retirement funds."

Get A Grip's Sharon Dillard started her company with savings and cash flow. But when it came time to purchase a new headquarters building, she and her management team took advantage of recently changed tax regulations that allowed them to use retirement savings to buy the property.

Then there's Graystone Industries' John Olson, who used retirement money to finance a move from a home garage to a warehouse. "It was a scary thing to do, but it has given us the freedom in life that a steady paycheck would never have," said John.

"If someone is starting their own business, they can either do it as a hobby with little investment in capital or they can throw caution to the wind and invest personally in its success," John continued. "I fully believe in working without a safety net. Fear is a great motivator, and the thought of being homeless living under a bridge keeps me creative and motivated instead of watching reruns of 'Gilligan's Island.' "

That approach often appeals to young, single entrepreneurs – and with good reason. When you have 40 or 50 years to recoup any financial losses, it may seem like a no-brainer to put retirement savings (if you have any) towards an untested, yet exciting startup with potential.

But it's harder to do this when you get older. Much harder, in fact.

"I started when my mortgage was paid off and my kids were grown," said Barbara Cosgrove of Barbara Cosgrove Lamps. "My husband and I had worked hard to get where we were. I didn't want to put us at risk."

Neither did David Drewry, the home inspection business owner who's now retired. That's why he was careful to keep his military pension separate from his business.

As an aspiring business owner, your best bet is to consult with a trusted financial advisor or two about your situation (more on that in a minute). Go ahead and ask about using retirement money towards your business. Just don't be surprised to hear that it isn't a good idea, since that's what they'll probably tell you.

So will the majority of successful late bloomers, who tend to take a measured, disciplined approach towards retirement – just like they do with the back end of their businesses. They spent *years* building their personal financial assets (like you, maybe) and don't want their entrepreneurial endeavor to drain the funds they'll need when (and if) they retire. That's the *last* thing they want, so they take steps to minimize that possibility.

GETTING OFF THE GROUND

Rather than tapping retirement accounts, many of the interviewed entrepreneurs used other financial sources to get themselves started. After the September 11, 2001 terrorist attacks occurred in TechGuard Security's second year, Suzanne Magee secured a low-interest $117,000 SBA loan that enabled the company to weather the post-tragedy recovery.

A few entrepreneurs used personal credit cards and/or took the smart step of borrowing money *before* they needed it. Prior to starting her full-time business, Donna Herrle arranged for a line of credit with a bank with a special division for women business owners. ABBA Associates' Bill Cheeks used a home equity line of credit established as a source of emergency funding, before he had plans to become an entrepreneur. "I believe it's important to have a reserve and have always operated that way," said Bill.

As this book neared completion, another financial source gaining momentum was crowdfunding, an online fundraising method that connects businesses with small investors. The more popular crowdfunding platforms include Kickstarter, Crowdfunder, Indiegogo and Peerbackers, to name just a few.

One business owner who's turned to crowdfunding is 89-year-old Pearl Malkin, the owner of Happy Canes. "Grandma Pearl," as many call her, enjoys her small business, a line of walking sticks that she decorates by hand with flowers. In 2013, she launched a Kickstarter campaign to raise $3,500 in startup capital.[4]

For those contemplating crowdfunding, research is a very good idea, of course. Scott Steinberg is the author of *The Crowdfunding Bible*, a comprehensive guide to raising money online. You can download the guide for free at www.crowdfundingguides.com

At some point, crowdfunding could become more mainstream among late-blooming entrepreneurs but the ones you're meeting didn't mention it. Instead, the majority provided their own startup funds or borrowed from family members. Remember Rory Kelly, the former steel industry executive who stashed away the bonuses he earned during his corporate years? Rory is proof that, by taking advantage of time and compound interest, disciplined savers can accumulate sufficient seed money on their own.

As you would expect, the dollar amounts vary, depending upon the type of business. While a one-person consulting practice may require little startup capital, the costs to open a franchise can be considerable. Just the initial fee paid to the franchisor to buy the business can range from a few thousand dollars to millions, depending upon the type and size of the franchise business.

For new small businesses, the median startup capital is about $50,000 for those with a payroll and $25,000 for those without one, says the U.S. Small Business Administration (SBA). Some entities get going with much less, however. The agency's data shows that a relatively large share of businesses (20 percent of employers and 39 percent of non-employers) uses less than $5,000 worth of startup financing.[5]

The SBA's figures seem consistent with the startup amounts for several of the late bloomers. Card Alert Services, for example, began with about

$40,000 provided by founders Richard Urban and Doug Anderson. At least one entrepreneur, however, far exceeded the SBA's statistics. When Suzanne Magee and her business partner, Andrea Johnson, began TechGuard Security, they tried unsuccessfully to obtain funding from venture capital firms. After regrouping, they went to family and friends and raised $300,000 in startup funds.

KEEPING YOUR FINANCIAL HOUSE IN ORDER

For many people, it's difficult enough just to secure the funding needed to start a business. But once it's up and running, the *real* money challenge begins.

"Expect to lose money your first year," said Prestige Limousine's Rory Kelly. "But figure out how to make money as you go along. Keep overhead to a minimum without sacrificing quality to the customer."

Simply put, you can't become profitable unless the business's financial side is in order. To make that happen, the late bloomers in this book stuck with a number of fundamentals.

GOOD FINANCIAL ADVISORS

Just about every interviewed business owner said this about accountants: Don't think about starting a business without a good one.

For entrepreneurs with no formal business training – which describes most of the people you're meeting – it wasn't enough to find someone who could prepare a balance sheet. For them, a "good" accountant is one who understands their business *and* gives them a strong comfort level.

To find someone who met those criteria, they often turned to their networks – which didn't always yield the right person on the first try. Graystone Industries' John Olson, for example, went through a few accountants – including one whose mistake resulted in an erroneous payment of several thousand dollars in taxes – before he found one he liked and trusted.

"It is so important to surround yourself with good financial experts and to form good, trusted relationships," said ABBA Associates' Bill Cheeks. "When I started the business, I sat down with two financial advisors. I continue to meet with these advisors on a quarterly basis. I believe it's worth getting, and paying for, financial advice."

TRACKING THE NUMBERS

"My least favorite part of the business is when someone doesn't pay or wants to return an order, even though it says on the terms sheet that we won't accept returns," said Annie Margulis, whose Girls Golf clothing line is mostly a business-to-business operation.

Even when things go right, bookkeeping is one of the least appealing aspects of business ownership for many entrepreneurs. Mention "cash flow" and their eyes glaze over. But successful entrepreneurs know you can't shirk this area. The financials, after all, tell you where you are and what you should do next.

"You need to look at sales on a daily, weekly, monthly and annual basis, to give you the data needed to make big-picture decisions," said Prestige Limo's Rory Kelly.

The numbers also tell you if something is wrong. Even with a competent financial team, you can't say to yourself: "Good, now I don't have to think about that anymore." Drawing Conclusions' Donna Herrle agrees.

"Too frequently, we hear of a trusted employee who did not manage the company's finances properly," she said. "It is perfectly fine to have an employee, or employees, handle that aspect, but do not lose sight of the details."

EXPENSE MANAGEMENT

Watching the numbers also means prudent management of the expense side – but as you heard from Bill Cheeks, many business owners have trouble doing this. Sharon Dillard has this simple advice: "Have a cap on expenses and adhere to it," she said. "Pay your bills on time. Don't spend more than you're bringing in."

That may not happen in the first year when, as noted by Rory Kelly, many businesses expect to lose money. To control or limit expenses, the business owners in this book relied upon a range of tactics. Here are some of them:

- *Bartering.* This can be a way for a cash-strapped startup to get much-needed products or support. As mentioned earlier, Heritage Memoirs' Jennifer Campbell used this approach, providing her editing skills in exchange for consulting services from a marketing coach.

- *Minimal overhead.* Most of the businesses in this book, including Barbara Cosgrove

Lamps, TechGuard Security and Get
A Grip, saved on rent by starting in
a garage, basement or other space in
their owners' homes. Some also avoided
employee health insurance, vacation
and other personnel expenses by hiring
independent contractors. Designing
Conclusions' Donna Herrle is among
those who use this approach to control
costs.

- *Help from family members.* Often, a
  sympathetic spouse pitches in and
  donates administrative or manual labor,
  especially at the beginning. Sometimes
  an entrepreneur is lucky enough to have
  relatives who can provide bookkeeping,
  marketing or other professional services
  that otherwise would be unaffordable
  for a brand new company (I was my
  husband's unofficial advertising manager
  for the first few years of his retail bicycle
  business).

- *Organic marketing.* Entrepreneurs use their
  existing networks to conduct their own
  product testing and market research,
  rather than pay big bucks for this service.
  In addition, those who have media-

relations skills, like RetiredBrains' Art Koff, use them to obtain exposure for their products or services.

- *Downsizing.* That's what Grace Welch and her husband, Marty, did when they relocated Patemm's headquarters from San Francisco to Rhode Island – a move that enabled them to get rid of "a big, fat mortgage," said Grace.

- *Doing without.* Entrepreneurs who succeed go through their share of lean or difficult times that require sacrifices, like cutting their own salary when circumstances warrant it. For some older entrepreneurs, especially those who come from high-paying corporate jobs, opening a business brings dramatic economic change. "If I had been younger, I would have been too focused on my material possessions," said St. Paul Great Harvest Bread Company's Bonnie Alton. "None of that matters anymore."

- *Eliminating frills.* When Cookies on Call's trucking company raised its prices, Franny Martin switched from glossy to flat-finish boxes – a way to offset the increase without affecting the quality of her cookies. She also sent personal letters to inform customers about the company's steps to avoid a price increase for its products.

While expense management is key, some entrepreneurs point out that it's possible to go overboard. "There's an opportunity cost to spending time on just expense reduction," said John Olson of Graystone Industries. Shopping for a cheaper trash-disposal service, for example, usurps time available to generate new customers or service existing ones.

CONTROLLED GROWTH

It's good to dream big, but entrepreneurs can get in trouble by trying to expand too quickly. If growth gets out of control, you won't be profitable. To the contrary, it will put you out of business.

For the business owners in this book, slow and steady wins the race. More often than not, they see themselves as marathon runners, rather than sprinters. Barbara Cosgrove, for example, takes care to introduce new product lines slowly, in part so she doesn't get ahead of her customers. Recognizing the lamp market has a ceiling, she's moved into other areas (specifically "home accents") – but again, at a slow pace.

While Get A Grip is proud to own its own head-quarters building, it didn't take that step until it was ready financially. "It was good to start slow and build the business to a place where we needed a showroom," said Sharon Dillard, Get A Grip's president.

THE RIGHT PRICING STRATEGY

For new business owners, what to charge can be a dilemma. Price your products or services too low and you may not make enough income, or be perceived as "cheap" in more ways than one. Price them too high and you may lose business to less expensive competitors.

Get A Grip is among the companies in this book that struggled with pricing initially. "We had to work our way into higher pricing gradually, knowing that some customers would be lost," said Sharon Dillard. "But we wanted the cream-of-the-crop customers – those who buy on quality and good work, not on price, because we do good work and have great products. We've never lowered pricing, and don't sell on price."

Graystone Industries' John Olson said the pond-supplies industry often sees new business owners who try to buy their customers with low prices. "These customers aren't loyal," he noted. "If they can find the product at a slightly lower price elsewhere, they're gone." His company has "fired" customers who are focused on price only by telling them: "I'm sorry, but we just can't help you."

"There's a subset of business that you're better off without," he added. "It's a fundamental that applies to all industries."

How do you find middle ground? Some entrepreneurs, like Donna Herrle, use data to determine their pricing. "I conduct or subscribe to market surveys to know where my business fits in the region, which tells me if I'm pricing profitably, where the demand is and what niche I can fill," she said.

"In the end, it comes down to what you're comfortable with, and the area where you live," said Heritage Memoirs' Jennifer Campbell. "Someone in Manhattan can charge more than someone in Toronto."

DON'T LOSE SIGHT OF WHAT REALLY MATTERS

This chapter may have surprised you since it contradicted common beliefs. In particular, it doesn't support the stereotypical image of an entrepreneur: a daring go-getter who's willing to bet the farm, or whatever personal financial assets exist, to achieve the dream of business ownership.

Sure, risk is inherent to entrepreneurship. And some late-blooming entrepreneurs *do* match the stereotype just described. But more often than not, they don't.

Most of the successful ones take careful steps to protect their retirement funds and minimize the odds of financial jeopardy. They have to because, unlike younger entrepreneurs, they don't have a big time window to recover from disastrous financial mistakes if they happen.

For that reason, they track expenses carefully, pay attention to the numbers, keep overhead to a minimum and, when possible, cut corners without sacrificing customer quality. They enlist good accountants whom they trust, control their expansion and develop the right pricing strategy.

By following these financial measures, they have sustainable businesses that let them pursue what matters to them personally. For Donna Herrle, that means leaving a legacy for the next wave of entrepreneurs. "I feel like part of my responsibility is to mentor the younger generation," said Donna. For that reason, she regularly hires design interns and plans to train additional graphic designers to take over her design business sometime in the future.

Heritage Memoirs' Jennifer Campbell has a similar view. Her two sons, both in their 20s, have other jobs for now, but she would love to see them take over her company one day. "I feel very proud," said Jennifer, "that I've shown them you can build your own business."

For Savvy Rest's Michael Penny, what matters is something discussed back in the chapter on customer service – having an authentic relationship with the customer.

"Profit should be a byproduct of your products' benefits and your relationship with your customers, not the goal itself," said Michael in a blog post that he penned for his company's website.

"I like profit, it's necessary for my business to thrive," he wrote. "But I don't want to hold dollar signs before my eyes. That's not how I want to live at home, at work, or at play."[6]

Maybe you feel the same way. Even if your top entrepreneurial objective isn't to become rich, you'll be better off implementing the same financial measures as the late bloomers. *Always watch the money.* By doing so, you're more likely to have a business that can thrive and support what matters to you personally – whatever it might be.

NOW WHAT? 10 WAYS TO TAKE ACTION

1. Choose a business idea that lets you to enjoy yourself *and* make a profit. Fulfillment of a passion and/or a sense of meaning may be driving you to become an entrepreneur. But you won't have a sustainable business that lets you achieve those things if you aren't making more money than you're spending.

2. Don't start your business without a good, trustworthy accountant. It's one of the most important hiring decisions you'll make on behalf of your business. Use your network to obtain referrals.

3. Evaluate your money-management behavior as part of your self-assessment. Most of the entrepreneurs in this book agree that your past payment history could be a predictor of your likely success as an entrepreneur. Use the quiz at the end of this chapter to help you gauge your financial tendencies.

4. Limit your credit use. Some late-blooming entrepreneurs avoided all debt because they didn't want to incur the risk. If you use credit, explore your borrowing options, which may include family loans, credit

cards and special financing programs from lenders. Evaluate the pros and cons of each option, then choose the one that makes the most sense for you.

5. Develop a pricing strategy. Base it upon your vision for the business, where it's located and whom you want as your customers, among other factors.

6. Keep your eye on the numbers. Determine how often you need to look at your financial reports, then set a schedule. Mark these dates on your calendar.

7. Start small and grow slowly. This will enable you to keep pace and avoid overextending yourself financially.

8. Control expenses without sacrificing quality. A combination of steps – such as taking advantage of home-based (and rent-free) office space, donated labor from family members and bartering – can help you get through lean times at the beginning. Even with these measures, expect to lose money during your first year.

9. Pay your bills on time! Don't spend more than you're bringing in! Too many business owners don't do these things, even though they're obvious steps towards profitability.

10. Be leery about any use of retirement funds. This presents a huge risk for someone over 40. Consult with a financial advisor before going this route.

ASSESSING YOUR PERSONAL FINANCE SKILLS

Answer yes or no for the following:

1. I have a monthly household budget.

2. I pay my household utility bills on time every month.

3. I've checked my credit report within the last twelve months.

4. I've never missed or been late on a mortgage or rent payment.

5. I've never bounced a check.

6. I have at least one retirement fund to which I've contributed regularly.

7. I have an emergency reserve fund to cover at least six months of living expenses.

8. I only use credit cards for convenience, not because I have to.

9. I pay the balance on my credit cards in full every month.

10. I've never declared personal bankruptcy.

Score:

8-10 yeses: You have a good handle on your finances

5-7 yeses: You'll need help in the money-management department.

0-4 yeses: Better think long and hard about whether you really want to run your own business.

CHAPTER 8
KEEP IT SIMPLE

If you want to succeed at entrepreneurship, don't try to be all things to all people. Pick one core product or service and do it well.

That approach works for Five Guys Burgers and Fries, a perennial favorite among *Washingtonian* magazine's readers and local "best burger" surveys. Five Guys began in 1986 as a single carry-out in Northern Virginia and quickly developed a cult-like following for its juicy hamburgers served on freshly baked buns. In 2003, the owners – Jerry and Janie Murrell and their five sons – began offering franchises and, in just 18 months, sold options for more than 300 units. Today, the company has more than 1,000 locations nationwide and more than 1,500 units in development.[1]

On the company's website, the Murrells attribute Five Guys' phenomenal growth to "their passionate and often fanatical focus on quality, service and cleanliness and their continual effort to keep things simple."[2] To implement this philosophy, they avoid fancy restaurant décors and feature a very short menu, which consists of little more than burgers (of course), fries, hot dogs and two or three sandwich options for vegetarians.

Five Guys' franchisee in Nashville, Tennessee, and Charlottesville, Virginia, is Bill McKechnie, who didn't get his start in the hamburger business until he was 46. In addition to an undergraduate degree from the University of Virginia, Bill has an MBA from the University of Chicago and a master's from the London School of Economics. He didn't go to business school with the intent of becoming an entrepreneur, however. "I was looking for the best generalist education I could get," he said.

After graduation, Bill went to New York City and became a securities analyst – a job he didn't like. He moved to the Washington, D.C. area to accept a position as director of finance and administration for a defense electronics firm.

During that time, Bill got his first taste of entrepreneurship when he became involved with a startup that provided training and logistics support for the defense industry. He enjoyed "the mechanics of starting something from scratch" but wasn't enamored with his industry, which "lacked a sense of product." He began searching for a new opportunity that would provide a passion.

That search led him to Great Harvest Bread Company. In 1993, he opened his own Great Harvest bakery in Alexandria, Virginia, where he adopted the company's mission to "be loose and fun, bake phenomenal bread, run fast to help customers, create strong, exciting bakeries, and give generously to others."[3]

Eleven years later, Bill sold the bakery and moved to Charlottesville, where he switched from bread to burgers when he opened his first Five Guys location in 2004. Two years later, he acquired Five Guys' Nashville territory, where he's opened four stores. Now in his 50s, Bill has plans for eight more locations in Nashville, giving him a total of 12 there in addition to three he operates in Charlottesville.

Bill has a clear vision developed from his years with two high-achieving franchise companies that are among the best (if not the best) in their respective product areas.

"I subscribe to the mantra that success can be found in simplicity," he said. "It's better to do something extremely well than a lot of things sort of well."

He isn't the only one who thinks this way. At

least one industry, financial services, designates a term ("monoline") for companies that choose to specialize in one area so they can become adept in all aspects of that offering. Entrepreneurs like Grace Welch (diaper-changing pads), Michael Penny (organic mattresses), David Drewry (home inspection services) and Franny Martin (cookies) also have built businesses by focusing on one core item or service and striving to become the best. From a product standpoint, they *keep it simple.*

If you're thinking about this type of approach for your business, more power to you. Just be aware that a single-focus model isn't easy to execute. As Bill McKechnie and other single-focus entrepreneurs will tell you, it took enormous amounts of time and energy to get to where they are today.

When you're a business whose success (and survival) depends upon one product area, superb execution of the basics is critical. So is a thorough understanding of your market and the real reasons why people buy your product or service. As you'll read in these pages, it takes discipline and hard work to stay focused on your business model, resist distractions – and become so good at what you do that your customers won't want to go anywhere else.

PRODUCT DIVERSIFICATION – A DOUBLE-EDGED SWORD

Businesses decide to diversify for many reasons. Here are some of them:

- *Survival.* A company in a shrinking industry or a saturated market may not be around very long if it doesn't diversify into new areas of growth.

- *Greater size or clout.* More product offerings can lead to more customers, as well as greater influence and bargaining power with suppliers.

- *Customer service.* A business may agree to order products outside its normal inventory to accommodate customers' requests.

- *Keeping up with the competition.* XYZ Company down the street starts offering a certain product, so a business owner thinks: "Maybe I'd better, too."

- *Wider exposure for a brand.* A business with a strong presence in one product area may diversify into others to augment its name recognition. A classic example is Virgin Group, whose brand name arose from a discount-record mail-order operation that founder Richard Branson started in 1970.[4] Today, the holding company's many business areas include travel, cell phone service and entertainment.

- *A need for a year-round revenue stream.* A seasonal business, such as an ice cream parlor or a ski shop, may be cash-strapped during off-peak months – so it diversifies into products or services to sell during these times of the year.

You don't have to be a conglomerate like AT&T or GE to benefit from diversification. Sometimes it can help a smaller business, especially when it's established itself in one area and adds another that's complementary to the first.

Drawing Conclusions' Donna Herrle is one example. In 2008, Donna acquired a second business, New Pittsburgh Publications, which she renamed Know Where to Go in Pittsburgh. The company sells around 20,000 printed materials annually to promote The Steel City, including an events calendar, *Rich/Poor Man's Guide to Pittsburgh* and a local walking map and guide.

Going from one to two companies was "very exciting," said Donna. The second was easier to open than the first, she said, in part because Know Where to Go in Pittsburgh is a seasonal business with ebbs and flows in its workload. As sister companies with similar labor needs, the two businesses can use the same subcontractors.

Before acquiring a second business, Donna thought about its interaction with her first. But what about entrepreneurs who don't have a solid expansion strategy and/or a first business that's established? They may encounter what legendary investor Peter Lynch described as "diworsification."[5] When that happens, it can create these problems:

- *A diluted focus.* "If I de-simplify and offer additional products in an effort to gather additional customers," Bill McKechnie asked rhetorically, "how much does that take my eye off the ball and risk losing my core customer and what I do well?"

- *Lack of familiarity.* This happens with the addition of a new product or service outside a core business. Entry into an unfamiliar area increases the odds for big mistakes, since you may not have the expertise needed to make sound judgments. Maybe that's why billionaire Warren Buffett, when he does media interviews, often says that he doesn't invest in businesses that he doesn't understand.

- *Spreading resources too thin.* Adding a new product or service takes time, money and energy. The burden might supersede any benefits derived from the diversification, especially for a new or small business.

- *Identity confusion.* Without a clear objective and a good marketing strategy, expanding into a new product area could leave your customers and employees wondering who you really are. A convoluted image is a big concern in the context of online shopping and Search Engine Optimization (SEO), whose goal is to boost a website's ranking within search results. When people look for something on the Web, they use specific terms to locate businesses that offer exactly what they need. How will they find yours if it has an unfocused identity?

WHY "KEEP IT SIMPLE" IS
HARDER THAN IT LOOKS

Given that any of these byproducts of diversification can destroy a business, most first-time entrepreneurs are better off with the Keep It Simple approach. One of its advantages is quality control, since it limits the number of support functions that require monitoring (the fewer products you offer, the fewer support functions you need). In contrast, a diversified company has to maintain high across-the-board standards of quality for *all* of its products, which can be complex and challenging.

Yet a different quality-related challenge emerges when you're a single-focus business. Unlike a diversified company, your bottom line depends on one core product. That adds pressure to be the best of the best, especially when you're in a product area (like hamburgers) where the customer has many choices and differentiation is blurred.

"If you stand for quality, you need to set a clear, recognizable standard to distinguish yourself – so that when it comes time for that customer to make a choice, only one name comes to mind," Bill McKechnie said.

While this strategy sounds straightforward, putting it in motion isn't. Some companies spend millions of dollars in an effort to create this type of distinction. Imagine the time and resources The Ritz-Carlton Hotel Company invested to develop its gold standard of customer service, now the benchmark for all kinds of businesses and the main reason for its hotels' unparalleled brand.

To become uncommonly good, you don't necessarily have to spend huge sums of money – but you *do* need a dedicated, comprehensive effort that aims for excellence in every facet of your business. That type of effort requires:

- *Attention to detail.* If you're the one manufacturing your core product, you have to pay attention to *everything* – from the equipment temperature to the quality of each individual ingredient. Five Guys, for example, uses only fresh ground meat and cooks its fresh-cut French fries in peanut oil.

- *Flawless execution.* In the days when he baked bread, Bill McKechnie used a simple recipe but followed it as closely as possible. No one jumps in and becomes the best baker – or the best wine producer, interior designer or whatever – right away. It takes time, repetition and persistence to master the basic procedures that provide the backbone of a great offering, per the 10,000-hours rule mentioned earlier. Even with a simple product or service, a lot can go wrong during the execution or assembly.

- *Systems.* Luxury-car dealer Carl Sewell addressed this topic in *"Customers for Life,"* his bestselling book on customer service. Businesses need "systems, not smiles," wrote Sewell, who believes systematic approaches are 80 percent of customer service.[6] The entrepreneurs featured in this book use systems as well, but they didn't develop them overnight. As mentioned earlier, Cookies on Call's Franny Martin tested the delivery of her products with several different shipping companies before she found one that met her standards. Systems take trial and error – and constant refinement.

In addition to the pressures associated with quality control, the Keep It Simple approach is harder than it looks for another reason: You have to be able to say no.

Unfortunately, some people can't seem to bring themselves to utter this two-letter response when they should. In an attempt to avoid confrontations, hurt feelings or added pressure, they may say yes and then later "forget" what they agreed to do.

But sometimes you *have* to say no to requests, offers and even some opportunities that could be distractions for your core business – or for you as an entrepreneur. "If you are doing things that don't move the ball, don't do them," said Tim Webb, the attorney whose story appeared in Chapter 2.

Likewise, the Keep It Simple approach also means saying no to people, projects or products that just aren't working. "I have only one rule: Always play to our strengths," said Barbara Cosgrove, the founder of Barbara Cosgrove Lamps. "If we have a lamp that is not doing well, we get out of it. We put our energy and focus on things that are working. That lesson plays over and over."

If you succeed with one product, vendors, suppliers and others who have profited from your success may urge you to expand. Grace Welch, who has done well with her Patemm diaper-changing pad, knows what this is like.

"We're a single-product company," said Grace. "But there's pressure to do more."

When a new product becomes "hot," a business may be tempted to jump on the bandwagon, especially when sales representatives offer favorable pricing terms and recount stories about competitors that have done well with the product. But if it doesn't fit into your plan, or you don't have objective marketing data to support the diversification, a trendy product can turn into a big mistake. Sometimes you have to say no – even when you want to say yes.

WHAT'S YOUR REAL BUSINESS?

On top of everything else, effective implementation of the Keep It Simple approach requires an understanding of your customers and the benefit(s) they derive from your core product. At first, this seems like a fundamental that any business would know. But sometimes, what people *really* want from a buying experience isn't as obvious as it seems.

Take the case of Licorice International, a Lincoln, Nebraska-based business that processes around 22,000 candy orders annually from its brick-and mortar shop and website. With 160 types from 14 countries, it has the largest selection of imported licorice in the U.S. Still, licorice isn't its true product, as you'll read in a minute.

In 2002, at ages 52 and 57 respectively, Elizabeth Erlandson and Ardith Stuertz, bought Licorice International, then a mail-order business, from a New York confectioner. They moved the company's headquarters from Manhattan to their hometown of Lincoln, where they developed a website and began filling orders from their homes.

It didn't take long for their business to flourish. By mid-2003, orders reached a level where the owners needed more space. Within three and a half years, Licorice International moved three times, adding a retail operation along the way. Its current location is a 4,450-square-foot facility with a store upfront.

Over the years, the company has had its challenges. While the recession affected its Internet business considerably, the retail shop has grown consistently. It now provides approximately 55 percent of total sales, which have increased fivefold since the business moved to its first commercial location in 2003.

Elizabeth and Ardith – known locally as "The Licorice Ladies"– attribute their business achievements to several factors, such as a strong work ethic, prudent fiscal management, a desire to learn and a good staff. In addition, these friends – who have known each other for more than 20 years – work well together and have complementary strengths. Elizabeth has marketing and communications expertise cultivated during 25 years as a professional writer. Ardith spent 23 years at a heavy-construction-equipment auction company, where she was responsible for the accounting and human resources departments.

What's also enabled Elizabeth and Ardith to succeed, however, is their in-depth knowledge about their clientele. Most of their customers were born between 1930 and 1960. Some are candy lovers with childhood memories of buying real licorice from the corner drugstore (most "licorice" candy sold in the U.S. these days actually gets its flavor from anise).

A visit to Licorice International's storefront, with its colorful displays of treats, brings back these pleasant memories. "Nostalgia is the real product we offer our customers," said Elizabeth. "They're 70 when they walk in the door and they're 10 when they walk out."

Most of the other entrepreneurs in this book see their product or service in the same light as Elizabeth and Ardith. In the end, they aren't offering diaper-changing pads, fraud-detection systems, golf clothes, organic mattresses or a hard-bound memoir. What they're *really* offering is something less tangible – a way to ease stress, peace of mind, a better self-image, improved health or a memory of a happy time. This realization serves as a guiding force for Keep It Simple entrepreneurs, helping them to operate their businesses in ways that produce what matters the most to their customers.

USING SELF-AWARENESS
TO STAY FOCUSED

As important as it is to know your product's true value for the customer, what's equally important is to know what matters most to you personally. This is a big deal for older entrepreneurs, as evidenced by the 2011 Civic Ventures/Met Life survey that found that the majority of potential "encore entrepreneurs" want to work on something that provides them with a sense of meaning.[7]

This desire for meaning could explain why a fair number of late bloomers do well by sticking with one core product or service. When your personal happiness and values are harmonious with those of your business, the Keep It Simple approach comes more easily.

One woman who knows this very well is Julie Savitt, an entrepreneur mentioned earlier. Julie is president and owner of AMS Earth Movers, a Lake Bluff, Illinois-based trucking company that hauls construction materials for roadways, parking structures, water-treatment plants, airports and other government and private-sector job sites throughout the Chicago area. Julie and her nine-member team also sell topsoil, road salt and other aggregate to government, commercial and residential clients.

In one respect, it's no surprise that the 46-year-old became a successful entrepreneur. Both of her parents owned businesses, as did her grandparents. As noted on her company's website, she grew up watching her grandfather help build Chicago.

In 2012, AMS Earth Movers had annual revenue of $3.2 million, a 23 percent increase from the previous year. Julie's accomplishments haven't gone unnoticed. In 2013, the Illinois District Office of the SBA named her Women in Business Champion of the Year. *Enterprising Women* magazine recognized her as one of its 2012 Enterprising Women of the Year award winners.

She's come a long way since 2004, when she founded AMS Earth Movers with her then-partner. For the first few years, they focused on serving as a resource for small businesses that were having difficulty getting off the ground.

In 2008, everything changed when her ex-partner had to leave the country. "I was 40 years old, with a mortgage to pay and three children near college," said Julie. Needing income, she considered looking for a corporate job, but "the prospect of joining the rat race was disenchanting," she said.

Instead, Julie looked at AMS Earth Movers in a different light. "I asked myself what I could do to make it something that's meaningful," she said. Her first step was six months of introspection to determine the answer.

To help with this self-assessment, Julie used a simple tool: a list written on a piece of paper taped to her bathroom mirror, a place that would ensure a daily look. She kept scratching off entries on the list and refining it until she was satisfied with the results.

"The hardest part," Julie added, "was figuring out what makes me happy. It's not a new car or other material possessions. It is the opportunity to learn every day and to work with people who have the same values that I do."

With that self-knowledge, Julie set her sights on remaking the business. Once she assumed control, she discovered unpaid debts. In addition, some customers – hearing rumors that AMS Earth Movers wouldn't survive under its new ownership – decided not to pay. The combined effect was a starting deficit of about $250,000, which took three years for Julie to recoup.

During that time, Julie became involved with the Cycle of Success Institute (COSi), a Chicago-based program with a 12-month process that teaches business owners how to transform their companies into profitable, high-growth businesses. Later, she participated in the Small Business Administration's

Emerging 200 Initiative, which selects 200 high-potential businesses from inner cities across the country to participate in a seven-month executive training program.

While both programs helped immensely, the foundation for AMS Earth Movers' growth came from Julie's resilience and the fundamentals that surfaced during her six months of self-analysis. Her priorities these days include recycling, conservation and other green initiatives as well as continuing education, a long-time passion. "I encourage my staff to seize opportunities to learn," she said. "It gives me joy to see them all grow and prosper."

"It's not all about sales," she continued. "It's also about educating people we work with. It is giving through sharing. That's what's generated our business."

Now that AMS Earth Movers is a Certified Woman-Owned Enterprise (CWE), Julie believes more strongly than ever in her company's original quest to extend a hand to small and minority-owned businesses. Among her volunteer causes is Heartland International, through which she hosted an intern from Kenya and traveled to that country to teach young entrepreneurs about sustainable business practices.

In five years, Julie wants to see her company

operate on a national level and become "a go-to company that sets standards." She also would like to expand beyond trucking one day and go into rail, barges and other types of commercial transportation.

It's been a tough road for Julie, but with life experience has come an understanding of what her business is really about. Thanks to the assessment she put herself through when she took control of AMS Earth Movers, she's able to stay focused on what matters the most.

"It used to be more about moving dirt," she said. "Now it's about good relationships and giving back."

WHERE LATE BLOOMERS HAVE AN ADVANTAGE

The Keep It Simple approach to start and build a business doesn't have any age limitations, of course. But if you're someone who's older, you may be better at it than a younger entrepreneur for a few reasons. As just discussed, the Keep It Simple approach becomes more doable when your business goals are aligned with what's most important to you – an understanding that comes with time.

In addition, a potential problem mentioned earlier – the inability to say no – sometimes decreases with age. The older you get, the more likely it is that you decline requests that don't interest you or absorb too much time. Often (but not always), those who have been around the block a few times learn that it's better to say no upfront, rather than to hem and haw.

While business owners have many ways to implement a Keep It Simple approach, some things will always be outside their scope of influence – a reality that late bloomers understand from experience. For entrepreneurs who are inventors, acceptance of this reality helps when dealing with one of quality control's more pernicious problems: cheap imitations. "Coming from the arts, I think the kiss of death is copying someone else," said Barbara Cosgrove of Barbara Cosgrove Lamps. "I see copies of my stuff in lower-end stores. But you don't waste your time on things you can't control."

Another reason why late bloomers may be better at applying the Keep It Simple approach is their tendency to choose business ideas with computer needs that are minimal and/or straightforward. Unlike the owners of multi-faceted or high-tech businesses, they usually don't have significant technical support requirements that create distractions and/or consume a lot of time.

To be clear, that's not to say that the technology

field doesn't have older entrepreneurs. Mention the phrase "tech entrepreneur" and most people think of Facebook's Mark Zuckerberg. Yet the notion that America's typical tech entrepreneurs are in their 20s is a myth, according to a 2009 survey of 549 company founders by Duke University. The survey found that the average and median ages of these founders was 40.[8] Tim Davis and Richard Urban, whom you met in earlier chapters, started their tech-related companies at ages 42 and 51, respectively.

But unless they're someone like Tim or Richard, with a technology background, late-blooming entrepreneurs typically gravitate towards businesses that meet a basic, everyday need or demand – such as food, home products/improvements, clothing or transportation services. Once in their core product area, they want to wow their customers with phenomenal service and quality. Sometimes this carries over to their branding. As mentioned in Chapter 2, Rory Kelly chose the name Prestige for his limousine business because it reflected the kind of service he wanted to provide.

Some of the tendencies and tactics discussed in early chapters also contribute to these entrepreneurs' ability to stay focused on a core product or service. Among them:

- *The use of contractors.* This allows business owners to delegate less-urgent and/or time consuming work so they can concentrate on quality and other key areas. One side benefit to the use of contractors: It also means fewer distractions from personnel problems, since it's easier to terminate contractors than employees when necessary.

- *A willingness to automate.* While they aren't always as tech savvy as their younger counterparts, late bloomers appreciate automation and the ways it can save time and streamline their operations. Even though his business has only a couple of employees, ABBA Associates' Bill Cheeks uses a payroll service, which lets him focus on other things instead of processing paychecks.

- *Limits on size and growth.* Sometime these limits apply to the early stages of a business. And sometimes they stay in place indefinitely. While Richard Urban and his business partner, Doug Anderson, founded Card Alert Services to address large-scale counterfeit ATM card fraud, that scope of work didn't carry over to the size of the organization. "I wasn't in it to build a big company," Richard said. "Neither of us wanted to manage a big staff."

AN APPROACH THAT BRINGS REWARDS

A Keep It Simple approach isn't the only path to entrepreneurial success. Many businesses, including some smaller ones, grow through diversification. But it wasn't the usual route taken by the late-blooming entrepreneurs interviewed for this book. Instead, they chose to excel in one core product or service area.

As mentioned in the last chapter, 40-and-older people often decide to become entrepreneurs to convert a single passion or interest into a business. That passion gives them sticking power and a willingness to devote time, energy and resources towards making their core product the best it can be.

If that's what you plan to do as well, great. To make a single-focus business work, however, you will have to avoid diversions, pay attention to details and implement systems that allow for consistent quality. You will need to know your business model – and stick with that model through thick and thin (or until circumstances tell you it's time to get out). At times, you will have to say no, even when you want to say yes.

None of those things is easy. But as you've seen from Five Guys and the other businesses discussed in this chapter, Keep It Simple is an approach that can bring rewards and gratification. It might even make you "the best of the best." Use that knowledge to keep yourself going.

NOW WHAT? 10 WAYS TO TAKE ACTION

1. Play to your strengths. If you want to adopt the "Keep It Simple" approach, choose a business that lets you concentrate – and excel – in one core product or service.
2. Dig deep to determine what business you're *really* in – and what your customers *really* want from you. The answer may not be as obvious as it seems.
3. Develop systems to ensure quality control. Once you know your systems, put them in a user-friendly operations manual for employees.
4. Read case studies about businesses well known for their dedication to quality. Identify lessons learned or "tricks of the trade" you can implement in your own business.

5. If a particular model or program isn't working, get out of it. Don't invest time or energy into trying to save it. Cut your losses and move on.

6. Say no when necessary. Don't give in to trendy or appealing offers that don't fit into your plan. Use objective marketplace data and customer feedback to guide your business decisions.

7. Limit technology upgrades to those that will help you focus on your core business and do it better. If an upgrade has the potential to be more trouble than it's worth, take a pass.

8. Diversify with care. Wait until you have a first business that's established and a solid expansion strategy. Size brings more complications that can make it difficult to Keep It Simple.

9. Learn about Search Engine Optimization (if you haven't already) so your business can apply it to market your core product area.

10. Use your passion to stay focused on your core product or service area. Remind yourself each day why your business matters so much to you.

CHAPTER 9
IN A NUTSHELL

The business owners in this book are proof that many of the best entrepreneurs out there are older than 40. Their contributions to the marketplace aren't limited in any way, either. As a group, they design clothing, protect cybersecurity, operate restaurants, provide car service, inspect homes, preserve family memories, lead self-improvement seminars, sell baked goods and run businesses in a host of other industries – all while maintaining a source of pride, gratification and income for themselves.

Each of the earlier chapters covered a principle that helped many of these entrepreneurs – all ordinary people like you and me – fulfill their dreams and start successful businesses in the second halves of their lives. Here's a recap of the eight principles, along with some key points for each one based upon what the featured entrepreneurs think and believe.

1. Go Out on the Right Limb

    * A willingness to take risks doesn't mean
      you have to accept *all* risks. To be a
      successful business owner, you have
      to take and manage certain risks while
      avoiding others.
    * Think long and hard about whether you
      have the tolerance for the uncertainty
      that lies ahead. It's an especially
      important question for 40-and older
      entrepreneurs who have a limited time
      window to recoup losses if they occur.
      And remember: It isn't just about you.
      You also have to think about the effects
      on family members.
    * The entrepreneurs in this book took
      advantage of opportunities brought
      about by luck. That doesn't mean,
      however, they took risks or made
      decisions about starting businesses
      based on the hope or belief they would
      get lucky.
    * A business plan's value lies in the
      critical thinking needed to put it
      together and the action steps taken to
      prevent problems *before* you encounter
      them.
    * An exit strategy decreases your risk of

things going wrong at the end. How you leave your business determines your ultimate success and profitability from the deal.

2. SWOT Yourself

   * A self-assessment is essential for all aspiring entrepreneurs, including those who are seasoned pros. In your eagerness to get going on your business, you may be tempted to skip this step. Don't. You can't manage your strengths and weaknesses if you don't know what they are.
   * Work experience, by itself, isn't enough for entrepreneurial success. The entrepreneurs who make it have a combination of traits that give them something extra. If you possess the right traits, a lack of technical expertise or formal professional credentials doesn't present an insurmountable weakness.
   * Passion, like professional experience, isn't always a strength by itself. You also need discipline to make key decisions about your business based upon facts and data, rather than what you desire or like personally. Without discipline, your

passion can become a major weakness,
with the potential to undo your business.
* Ability gaps are facts of life for all
business owners. The best ones
acknowledge these gaps and find ways to
offset them. The sooner you identify your
weaknesses (and take action), the better.

3. Make It a Family Affair
* Rather than "this is my deal," late
bloomers see their entrepreneurial
endeavors as package deals – where
their families are very much part of the
equation.
* Even if they don't have young kids,
entrepreneurs in the 40-and-older age
bracket may be susceptible to family
pressures for another reason: They've
been around long enough to accumulate
complex or extended family situations
involving more dependents.
* Successful late-blooming entrepreneurs
tend to have entrepreneurial spouses/
partners or come from entrepreneurial
families, a history that provides several
advantages. For one thing, these business
owners had witnessed and, to some

degree, already lived the ups and downs of entrepreneurship by the time they started out on their own.

* Aside from obtaining family buy-in, the most important way late-blooming entrepreneurs can manage family pressures is through effective time management.
* Make it part of your pre-launch research to determine what level of family involvement will benefit your startup. More often than not, people don't think about this question upfront, in part because they're focused on other things and assume the family stuff will work itself out.

4. Know Who You Need to Know

* You're far more likely to get better results with a deliberate approach to networking, rather than a "networking just happens" style.
* Established business owners use their networks to meet both immediate and long-range strategic objectives.
* Your personal network should have both in-person and social media contacts, even

if you're still figuring out the latter.
* Established entrepreneurs tend to have a
genuine desire to help others, especially
aspiring business owners.
* If you take the initiative and reach out to
these entrepreneurs, you're likely to be
rewarded – as long as you remember this:
It shouldn't be all about you. Be willing
and prepared to offer help in return. In
many situations, NetWeaving may be a
better approach than networking.
* Networking should be a constant process.
As your business evolves, so will the
expertise you need. Expect to devote time
to augmenting your network, as well as
renewing some of your old acquaintances.

5. Be Neighborly

* For late bloomers, the drive for great
customer service comes from something
that can't be taught in a seminar. The
biggest influence and motivator is their
life-long experience as a customer.
They've seen the good, the bad and the
ugly of customer service and they know,
from firsthand experience, what makes
customers happy and unhappy.

* For businesses, the neighbor comparison works two ways. It means not only *treating* customers the same way as a neighbor but *being* one as well. That dual role comes easily to late bloomers, who have a tendency to embrace humanitarianism.

* Despite the absence of physical contact with customers, an online business can offer neighborly customer service – but it needs to pay attention to the tone of its visual, written, verbal and electronic communications.

* To succeed in providing a great experience for their customers, entrepreneurs have to think holistically and pay attention to aspects of their business that the public never sees (and doesn't care about). These behind-the-scenes aspects include the business owner's relationships with vendors and employees.

* In the end, treating your customer like your neighbor means exactly that – extending hospitality, reliability, personal attention and warmth to make customers feel a certain way. The basics are the basics. Treat people the same way *you* want to be treated.

6. Stay on the Tiger

  * Successful business ownership is an achievement that requires a sustained, focused effort over time. A brand doesn't happen overnight. In most cases, it takes a lot longer than you think.

  * Aspiring entrepreneurs may not last because they're unwilling to commit to the marathon effort that's normally required before any real money comes in. They underestimate the difficulties and the time it takes to go from a negative to a positive cash-flow situation.

  * Time management helps – a lot. Remember Tim Webb's comments back in Chapter 2? He's a big proponent of the 80-20 principle – i.e., spend 80 percent of your time on the 20 percent that matters the most. That step alone will go a *long* way to help any entrepreneur achieve key goals.

  * An ability to focus gives you a big advantage when it comes to completing both long-term goals and everyday tasks.

7. Watch the Money

  * For many late-blooming entrepreneurs,

the No. 1 goal isn't to make big bucks. It's about enjoying what you're doing and getting the most out of what life has to offer.

* Any entrepreneur who wants to succeed has to care about profitability. You can't achieve any of your entrepreneurial goals if the math doesn't work – i.e., you aren't making more money than you're spending.

* Businesses tend to reap financial rewards when their owners care about lifestyle and treat those around them accordingly.

* Plenty of people – including those who are 40 or older and own businesses – never master personal finance basics. It's a good idea to gauge your personal finance behavior since it could indicate your odds for success as a business owner.

* When you're young and single, it may seem like a no-brainer to put retirement savings (if you have any) towards an untested, yet exciting startup with a lot of potential. It becomes a lot harder to do this when you're older – a reality that highlights a key difference between younger and older entrepreneurs.

* Don't think about starting a business without a good accountant. Find one who understands what you do and gives you a strong comfort level.

8. Keep It Simple

* If you're thinking about a single-focus approach for your business, more power to you. Just remember: It isn't easy to execute. As other single-focus entrepreneurs will tell you, it takes enormous amounts of time and energy to do it right.
* Diversification can help smaller businesses, especially when they've established themselves in one area and add another that's complementary to the first. For the entrepreneur who doesn't have a good expansion strategy and/or a first business that's on solid ground, diversification can create problems.
* To become uncommonly good, you don't have to spend huge sums of money – but you do need a dedicated, comprehensive effort that aims for excellence in every facet of your business. You also have to be able to say no when necessary. That's

something that many people can't, or
don't, do.

* The Keep It Simple approach requires
an understanding of your customers
and the benefits they derive from your
core product. At first, it seems like a
fundamental that any business would
know. But sometimes, what people really
want from a buying experience isn't as
obvious as it seems.

* It's also important to know what matters
the most to you personally. When your
personal happiness and values are
harmonious with those of your business,
the Keep It Simple approach becomes
easier.

* Keep It Simple is an approach that can
bring rewards and gratification. It might
even make you "the best of the best." Use
that knowledge to keep yourself going.

CHAPTER 10

WORDS OF WISDOM FROM LATE-BLOOMING ENTREPRENEURS

Successful entrepreneurship depends upon many factors, but the principles that serve as the underpinning for this success aren't mysterious or complicated.

From the international corporations renowned for their exemplary service to the entrepreneurs you've met in these pages, the best businesses use tried-and-true basics that never go out of style, even with the advent of new technology, revolutionary products and other changes that alter customers' lifestyles. There's no reason these principles can't help any aspiring business owner, regardless of age.

What, then, is distinctive about late-blooming entrepreneurs and the way they achieve their business success? *It's their collective life experience.* For just about every business featured in this book, this was the biggest success factor.

Here's what some late bloomers had to say about why life experience matters so much:

"Life experience brings a lot to the business table. Because of my age, I didn't have to look for people to do things because I knew them already. By the time you're 45, you know certain things."

Barbara Cosgrove, Barbara Cosgrove Lamps

"No, I could not have done this in my 20s. There's this belief in the Jewish religion that you don't really know what you want, or who you are, until you are 40. It took the first 40 years of experiences to identify the strengths and weaknesses that define who I am today. That self-understanding gives me the stamina to endure."

– Julie Savitt, AMS Earth Movers

"My age was more of a positive than a negative factor. Life experience has helped me tremendously. It drove me to entrepreneurship."

– Suzanne Magee, TechGuard Security

"I don't think I could have done this when I was younger. I didn't have the relationships and the

network that I have now. I also needed the experience I got working in a corporation."

– Tim Davis, Zalex

"Had I started my business 15 years earlier, I might have had the courage, but I would not have progressed the same way."

– Donna Herrle, Drawing Conclusions

"In my 20s, I probably would not have been as successful because I didn't have this stamina. Back then, I didn't have the financial resources and I didn't have the focus. Also, I don't think I would have been as open to as many ideas – and wouldn't have been able to take the ups and downs. It takes experience and maturity."

– Annie Margulis, Girls Golf

"Certainly, being older brought with it the wisdom that comes with age and work experience. It also brought a sense of realism in terms of setting and achieving goals."

– Sharon Dillard, Get A Grip

"I could not have run a company as a younger man. I did not have the experience or wisdom. It took years of working to cultivate the kind of customer service expertise I have now."

— John Olson, Graystone Industries

Wow. Just look at all these advantages! More drive. Sufficient financial resources. Knowledge. Focus. Experience. Maturity. Better networking skills. More relationships. More openness towards new ideas. The resilience to deal with ups and downs. A sense of realism when setting goals. A different way to progress. A better understanding of what you want, and who you are.

It's quite a list, isn't it?

John Olson's comment about customer service is especially significant. Any competent business owner can adopt policies that instruct employees to greet each customer or resolve service problems promptly. But when you can inject the sincerity, empathy, desire, knowledge and judgment that come from being a customer yourself for 40 years or more, your customers feel it. It takes your business to a whole other level.

Life experience enables late bloomers to do a better job of executing the fundamentals that are behind all great businesses. Keep this in mind as you move forward.

It's what you'll need to do and, as someone who possesses life experience, *can* do, to stand out from the crowd.

Here's one other key question: If the principles for entrepreneurial success are simple, why do so many small businesses fail within their first years of operation? Chapter 6 highlights one reason: Would-be business owners often underestimate, or lack, the discipline and tenacity required to stay the course and follow through. In the words of Girls Golf's Annie Margulis, "A lot of people have ideas but they don't implement them. You have to stick with it."

That's something else to remember for the days ahead. Right now, as someone who's just starting – or thinking about starting – a business, you may be running on a high level of adrenaline. But even if you possess drive and determination, it will be tough to sustain that level day in and day out. So let me offer two things that could help.

One is a tip given to me during an informational interview I conducted when I decided to write about late-blooming entrepreneurship. It comes courtesy of the CEO of a multi-million-dollar company in the automotive industry.

When I met with this executive, I expected the conversation to be about the book and his views on what it ought to include. Instead, he turned the tables and quizzed me about my personal reasons for writing the book. His advice to me was this: Write these reasons on a piece of paper that you'll see every day.

"As you get into your book, you'll have days when writing isn't fun," he said. "You'll want to quit. Having your reasons in front of you will help keep that from happening."

Boy, was he right. In the four years it took me to research and write the manuscript, I had days when I sat at my computer for hours and couldn't find the right words. I had days when I wrote and re-wrote the same paragraph several times, and still wasn't satisfied. During those times, it helped – tremendously – to have a written reminder of why I was putting myself through all this "fun."

You can do the same thing by going back and re-examining your reasons for wanting to have your own business. For this to work, you have to go beyond the surface and tap into the emotion of why these reasons matter – *really* matter – to you personally.

For example, it isn't enough to say "I want to be my own boss." Maybe it's "I want to give myself the freedom to pursue projects I want to do, not what someone tells me to do" or "I want to control my own schedule to ensure I spend time each day with my kids and never miss their soccer games (or whatever activity matters the most to them)." Whatever compels and drives you, *put it in writing*. Like AMS Earth Movers' Julie Savitt, it may take a few tries before you finally capture your reasons. Once you do, place them where you'll see them every day.

On that note, this final chapter includes a second item intended to help when you're having an off day. It's a selection of quotes from the entrepreneurs interviewed for this book. Some of these "Words of Wisdom" appear elsewhere in these pages while others you'll see for the first time. Read through them for some thoughts on what it takes to achieve success and get through difficult times as well as what makes entrepreneurship worthwhile. I hope that some, or maybe many, of these quotes give you a lift when you need one.

Don't let anyone tell you that you're "too old" to have a successful business. To the contrary, life experience gives you a big edge and may open opportunities that weren't available to you earlier. Like any entrepreneur, you'll have to work smart, work hard and make sacrifices without any guarantees (in business or in life, there aren't any except death and taxes). But if you follow the principles used by other late-blooming entrepreneurs, you can increase your odds for success as a business owner. Good luck!

WHAT IT TAKES TO ACHIEVE SUCCESS

"Hard work, non-compromising product quality and luck have an awful lot to do with success. In my case, I was fortunate to meet the right people at the right time, who gave me the right advice."

– Franny Martin, Cookies on Call

"There's no perfect way to run a business. It's never easy. You learn from your mistakes."

– Grace Welch, Patemm.

"You put yourself out there and that's the luck. You have to be open to other possibilities constantly. "

– Barbara Cosgrove, Barbara Cosgrove Lamps

"I focused on something that I enjoy doing – and that I'm good at doing."

– Tim Davis, Zalex.

"A lot of people have ideas but they don't implement them. You have to stick with it. A brand doesn't happen overnight."

– Annie Margulis, Girls Golf

"Dream big. Do the best work you can possibly do. Don't rest on your laurels. You have to set the bar as high as you possibly can."

– Jennifer Campbell, Heritage Memoirs

"Choose partners who are not like you, to ensure a diversity of strengths, talents and leadership styles that make a winning team."

– Suzanne Magee, TechGuard Security

"I'm not afraid of working hard and have never had the idea that I would stop at some point."

– Bonnie Alton, Great Harvest Bread Company – St. Paul, Minn.

"Always answer your telephone and say yes – then do what you said you would do."

– Rory Kelly, Prestige Limousine

"Be aboveboard, professional, reliable and timely. Be all the things you would expect from a professional."

– David Drewry, Drewry Home Inspections

"It takes a good idea and having someone who knows whatever you don't know. Don't start a business until you know basic accounting or someone you trust deeply knows it."

– Michael Penny, Savvy Rest

"To run your own business, you don't need a four-year degree in computer science. But you need an understanding of consumer trends that relate to your industry. I know my customers, I know my products and I know my marketing. That's what matters the most."

– John Olson, Graystone Industries

"Values are very important. You have to align yourself with the people who value the same things that you do."

– Julie Savitt, AMS Earth Movers

"Do not be afraid to fail."

— Richard Urban, Card Alert Services

"Much of success is about paying attention and getting the details right. As you increase your scope and size, you must have systems in place that will still allow you to nail the details."

– Bill McKechnie, Erewhon

"Self-marketing is a critical skill for entrepreneurs. Be prepared to sell yourself."

– Donna Herrle, Drawing Conclusions

"Get organized and find the best people for your business. Those two things have helped me the most."

– Sharon Dillard, Get A Grip

"Be willing to work hard. Nobody else cares about your business as much as you do."

– Elizabeth Erlandson, Licorice International

GETTING THROUGH DIFFICULT TIMES

"There were really lean times at the beginning. When you're in it for the long haul, you understand peaks and valleys."

– Jennifer Campbell, Heritage Memoirs

"You have to be tough. You have to be ready to deal with it and have emotional support."

– Michael Penny, Savvy Rest

"If my back starts to hurt, I pretend it doesn't. I just keep my eye focused. It's really about mental focus."

– Franny Martin, Cookies on Call

"A key question is whether there's a family commitment. If it's not there, how's that commitment going to run into your business? You need to have that support system."

– Grace Welch, Patemm

"Expect to lose money your first year. Keep overhead to a minimum without sacrificing quality to the customer."

— *Rory Kelly, Prestige Limousine*

"Reach out. Find a mentor. Entrepreneurs want to give back."

— *Suzanne Magee, TechGuard Security*

"I just pace myself. I have a lot of great people who help. You just roll with the punches."

— *Barbara Cosgrove, Barbara Cosgrove Lamps*

"You have to be open to change."

— *David Drewry, Drewry Home Inspections*

"If you have an idea, you have to be able to work hard, persevere, listen to people and still stay true to yourself. Don't be discouraged."

— *Annie Margulis, Girls Golf*

"Everyone makes mistakes when starting out. If you start small, these mistakes are not likely to be expensive ones."

— *Art Koff, RetiredBrains.com*

"Being physically fit gives you discipline. It takes a certain amount of tenacity to keep running when you're hurting. Those traits carry over to starting a business."

— Bonnie Alton, Great Harvest Bread Company — St. Paul, Minn.

"You have to love what you do, then those challenges become good challenges. Never stop learning."

— Julie Savitt, AMS Earth Movers

"Whenever we were over our heads, we found the right experts, such as attorneys who specialized in franchising, public relations/marketing experts and accountants. Leveraging the expertise of others is key to any successful business."

— Sharon Dillard, Get A Grip

"Any entrepreneurial endeavor requires large amounts of time and energy. You had better be willing to make those commitments if you want to enter that environment. Otherwise, you're better off staying out of it."

— Bill McKechnie, Erewhon

WHAT MAKES ENTREPRENEURSHIP WORTHWHILE

"It's not a new car or other material possessions. For me, it is the opportunity to learn every day and to work with people who have the same values that I do. It's giving my children a happy, healthy life, helping my staff grow and having time to smell the roses."

— Julie Savitt, AMS Earth Movers

"I want to enjoy the free time and the lifestyle that I have. The best part is I get to stay home with my family. I've also been able to free up other people so they can enjoy the same type of lifestyle."

— John Olson, Graystone Industries

"I enjoy cultivating long-term relationships and the feeling that I'm providing a service that people appreciate."

— David Drewry, Drewry Home Inspections

"My favorite part is seeing someone wearing one of my own outfits. It's very exciting."

– Annie Margulis, Girls Golf

"The most gratifying aspect? Working with people – and seeing the employees work to their capacity."

– Richard Urban, Card Alert Services

"I want to leave a legacy for my sons. I feel very proud that I've shown them you can build your own business."

– Jennifer Campbell, Heritage Memoirs

"I'm happy with my life and want to keep doing what I'm doing. When I worked in law, it was important to me to have a new corporate suit each month. Now, my biggest decision is what color Great Harvest T-shirt I'm going to wear with my black slacks."

– Bonnie Alton, Great Harvest Bread Company – St. Paul, Minn.

ACKNOWLEDGMENTS

Many people helped with this book but I especially wanted to thank the following:

Tom Durkin, Mike Kane, Art Koff, Kathy McKay, Fran Smith, Bruce Summers, Richard Urban and Tim Webb, who took the time to read some or all of the manuscript drafts and offer comments. Their feedback made the final product so much better.

Dave Conti, a manuscript editor and an authority on business-book publishing whose suggestions greatly improved the book's organization, content and style.

Nancy McKeon, a talented editor and writer who copyedited the text. I'm grateful for her keen eye.

Janet Flynn, a retired communications executive and good friend, who provided input and encouragement from start to finish.

My mother, Gerry Freehof, whose wise advice was to emphasize the independence and joy associated with being a late-blooming entrepreneur.

Sean and Erin, who put up with their mother writing this book.

And my husband and strongest supporter, Jim Strang, who happens to be the savviest entrepreneur I know.

SUGGESTED RESOURCES

Shown below is a list of organizations that have information of interest to older entrepreneurs:

AARP – Among other things, has a public discussion group dedicated to entrepreneurship on its website. www.aarp.org

Center for Productive Longevity – Serves as a bridge between employers seeking needed talent and people age 55 and older who have the capabilities and desire to continue working with employers as well as in entrepreneurial or other activities. www.ctrpl. org

Cycle of Success Institute (COSi) – Educates, coaches and transforms small to mid-sized companies into profitable, innovative, high-growth businesses that fuel job creation and wealth. www.cycleofsuccess. net

Encore.org (formerly Civic Ventures) –This group "is building a movement to make it easier for millions of people to pursue encore careers – second acts for the greater good." www.encore.org

Ewing Marion Kauffman Foundation – The world's largest foundation dedicated to entrepreneurship. www.kauffman.org

Franchise Direct – An online portal of franchise opportunities and information. www.franchisedirect.com

National Federation of Independent Business – Includes resources on starting a business, financing and accounting, etc. www.nfib.com

RetiredBrains.com – An independent job and information resource for boomers, retirees and people planning their retirement. www.retiredbrains.com

Senior Entrepreneurship Works – Helps those age 50 and older build sustainable businesses, create jobs and stimulate economic self-reliance. www.seniorentrepreneurshipworks.org

SCORE – Provides free counseling, resources and advice to people who are in business or want to start a business. Website materials include templates for business plans and financial statements. www.score.org

U.S. Chamber of Commerce Small Business Nation – A community that "was founded on the open exchange of information and ideas, while creating the opportunity for small businesses to speak with a unified voice." www.uschambersmallbusinessnation.com

U.S. Small Business Administration – Provides loans, loan guarantees, contracts, counseling sessions and other forms of assistance to small businesses. Website materials include templates and step-by-step guides for writing a business plan. www.sba.gov

OTHER PUBLICATIONS THAT MAY BE OF INTEREST:

Mature Entrepreneur Planning Guide, NYS Small Business Development Center, The State University of New York. www.nyssbdc.org/resources/Publications/09_mature_entrepreneur_planning_guide.pdf

BoomerPreneurs – How Baby Boomers Can Start Their Own Business, Make Money and Enjoy Life, M.B. Izard.

www.consultach.com/boomerpreneurs

Second Acts – Creating the Life You Really Want, Building the Career You Truly Desire, Stephen M. Pollan and Mark Levine.

ABOUT THE AUTHOR

Lynne Strang is, herself, a late bloomer. In 2010, she retired from her "real job" of 17 years to become a communications consultant, freelance writer and book author. Her blog, Late-Blooming Entrepreneurs, covers topics of interest to aspiring and new entrepreneurs who are 40 and older. Previously, she was Vice President of Communications for a financial services trade association, where she wrote about credit issues affecting consumers and small businesses. She lives with her family in Northern Virginia. To reach Lynne, please send her an email at lbstrang@gmail.com.

NOTES

Chapter 1: Go Out on the Right Limb

1. Vivek Wadhwa, Raj Aggarwal, Krisztina "Z" Holly and Alex Salkever. "The Anatomy of an Entrepreneur: Making of a Successful Entrepreneur," Ewing Marion Kauffman Foundation, November 2009, 6 http://www.kauffman.org/~/media/kauffman_org/research%20reports%20and%20covers/2009/07/makingofasuccessfulentrepreneur.pdf

2. "Get Ready," U.S. Small Business Administration (SBA) Small Business Planner, accessed October 13, 2010, http://2008.myvote.org/www.sba.gov/smallbusinessplanner/plan/getready/serv_sbplanner_plan_whatittake.html.

3. Paul Morin. "Are entrepreneurs gamblers?" *CompanyFounder* (blog), August 24, 2011, http://www.companyfounder.com/2011/08/are-entrepreneurs-gamblers/.

4. "Life Expectancy by Sex, Age, and Race: 2008," U.S. Census Bureau, Statistical Abstract of the United States, 2012, http://www.census.gov/compendia/statab/2012/tables/12s0104.pdf.

5. Seth Levine. "Is there an age bias in venture capital?" *Seth Levine's VC Adventure* (blog), October 12, 2011, http://www.sethlevine.com/wp/2011/10/is-there-age-bias-in-vc-investing.

6. "How to Write a Business Plan," SBA, http://www.sba.gov/content/how-write-business-plan-1.

7. Business plan template, SCORE, http://www.score.org/resources/business-plan-3.

8. Ibid.

Chapter 2: SWOT Yourself

1. Wadwha et al., "The Anatomy of an Entrepreneur," 5.

2. Sam Walton with John Huey. *Sam Walton, Made in America: My Story* (New York: Doubleday, 1992), 35.

3. "Get Ready," SBA Small Business Planner.

4. Laura Petrecca. "Seven famous founders share money mistakes, smart moves," *USA Today*, updated September 28, 2009, http://usatoday30.usatoday.com/money/smallbusiness/startup/week3-famous-founders.htm.

CHAPTER 3: MAKE IT A FAMILY AFFAIR

1. "Joan Lunden, 54, mother of twins," NBCNews.com, updated May 19, 2004, http://www.nbcnews.com/id/5014340/.

2. Ellen Galinsky, Kerstin Aumann and James T. Bond. "Times Are Changing: Gender and Generation at Work and at Home," Families and Work Institute, 2008 National Study of the Changing Workforce, revised August 2011, 19, http://familiesandwork.org/site/research/reports/Times_Are_Changing.pdf.

3. Wawha et al., "The Anatomy of an Entrepreneur," 6.

CHAPTER 4: KNOW WHO YOU NEED TO KNOW

1. Wadwha et al., "The Anatomy of an Entrepreneur," 5.

2. The White House, Presidential Decision Directive/NSC-63, May 22, 1998, http://www.fas.org/irp/offdocs/pdd/pdd-63.pdf.

Chapter 5: Be Neighborly

1. Jay MacDonald. "Car insurance company trivia: State Farm," Bankrate.com, March 29, 2013, http://www.bankrate.com/finance/insurance/car-insurance-company-trivia-state-farm.aspx.

2. "Disney World Good Neighbor Hotels," OrlandoVacation.com, accessed August 1, 2013, http://www.orlandovacation.com/hotels/disney-world-good-neighbor-hotels/.

3. "Fred Rogers," The Biography Channel website, accessed July 30, 2013, http://www.biography.com/people/fred-rogers-9462161.

4. Kathy Mance. "L.L. Bean President shares secrets to top-notch service," National Retail Federation, Retail's BIG Blog, September 14, 2010,

http://blog.nrf.com/2010/09/14/l-l-bean-president-shares-secrets-to-top-notch-customer-service/.

5. "The Ritz-Carlton: About Us: Gold Standards," accessed July 30, 2013, http://corporate.ritzcarlton.com/en/About/GoldStandards.htm.

CHAPTER 6: STAY ON THE TIGER

1. Angela L. Duckworth, Christopher Peterson, Michael D. Matthews and Dennis R. Kelly. "Grit: Perseverance and Passion for Long-Term Goals." *Journal of Personality and Social Psychology*, 2007, 1098, http://www.sas.upenn.edu/~duckwort/images/Grit%20JPSP.pdf.

2. Ibid, 1098.

3. Malcolm Gladwell. *Outliers: The Story of Success*, paperback edition (New York: Bay Back Books/Little, Brown and Company, 2011), 40.

4. Lynne Strang. "What Barbie, Bifocals and Barbed Wire Have In Common," *Late-Blooming Entrepreneurs* (blog), September 29, 2011,

http://latebloomingentrepreneurs.
wordpress.com/2011/09/29/what-barbie-
bifocals-and-barbed-wire-have-in-common/

5. Stephen J. Dubner and Steven D. Levitt.
"The Stomach-Surgery Conundrum," *The
New York Times*, November 18, 2007,
http://www.nytimes.com/2007/11/18/
magazine/18wwln-freakonomics-t.html?_r=1.

6. Duckworth et al., "Grit," 1091-92.

7. Nick Schulz. "Steve Jobs: America's Greatest
Failure," *National Review Online*, August 25,
2011,
http://www.nationalreview.com/
articles/275528/steve-jobs-america-s-
greatest-failure-nick-schulz.

CHAPTER 7: WATCH THE MONEY

1. "Encore Entrepreneurs: Creating Jobs,
Meeting Needs," Encore.org (formerly Civic
Ventures). Study conducted by Penn Schoen
Berland, released November 2011,
http://www.encore.org/files/
EntrepreneurshipFastFacts.pdf.

2. "Bankruptcy Filings Decline in Calendar
Year 2012," Administrative Office of the U.S.
Courts, February 4, 2013,

http://news.uscourts.gov/bankruptcy-filings-decline-calendar-year-2012.

3. "TransUnion: Credit Card Delinquencies and Debt Open 2013 with Declines," May 21, 2013, http://newsroom.transunion.com/press-releases/transunion-credit-card-delinquencies-and-debt-ope-1019129#.UfkRPatvLb0.

4. Parija Kavilanz. "89-Year-Old Grandma's Startup on Kickstarter," *CNNMoney*, February 20, 2013, http://money.cnn.com/2013/02/20/smallbusiness/grandma-kickstarter-startup/index.html.

5. "Frequently Asked Questions about Small Business Finance," SBA Office of Advocacy, September 2011, http://www.sba.gov/sites/default/files/files/Finance%20FAQ%208-25-11%20FINAL%20for%20web.pdf.

6. Michael [Penny]. "Selfless Selling: A Manufacturer's View," Savvy Rest Blog, January 13, 2012, http://www.savvyrest.com/blog/selfless-selling.

Chapter 8: Keep It Simple

1. "About Us: The Five Guys Story," Five Guys Burgers and Fries, accessed July 31, 2013, http://www.fiveguys.com/about-us.aspx.

2. "Five Guys Burgers and Fries" (franchise brochure), accessed July 31, 2013, http://www.fiveguys.com/media/3472/real_estate_packet.pdf.

3. Great Harvest Bread Company, Company History, accessed July 31, 2013, http://www.greatharvest.com/company/history.html.

4. Virgin Group, Company History, accessed July 31, 2013, http:www.virgin.com/history.

5. Definition of "Diworsification," Investopedia.com, accessed July 31, 2013, http://www.investopedia.com/terms/d/diworsification.asp.

6. Carl Sewell and Paul B. Brown. *Customers for Life: How to Turn That One-Time Buyer into a Lifetime Customer,* paperback edition (New York: Crown Business, 2002), 27.

7. "Encore Entrepreneurs: Creating Jobs, Meeting Needs," Encore.org (formerly Civic Ventures).

8. Vivek Wadwha. "Five Myths About Entrepreneurs," *The Washington Post,* July 29, 2011, http://articles.washingtonpost.com/2011-07-29/opinions/35266800_1_entrepreneurs-venture-capitalists-silicon-valley.

INDEX

CPSIA information can be obtained at www.ICGtesting.com
Printed in the USA
BVOW07s1806290615

406663BV00015B/415/P

9 780989 980326